Faith Hill

Other Music Books by James L. Dickerson

Colonel Tom Parker
The Curious Life of Elvis Presley's Eccentric Manager

Dixie Chicks
Down-Home and Backstage

Women on Top
*The Quiet Revolution That's Rocking the
American Music Industry*

That's Alright, Elvis
*The Untold Story of Elvis's First Guitarist and
Manager, Scotty Moore*
with Scotty Moore

Goin' Back to Memphis
A Century of Blues, Rock 'n' Roll and Glorious Soul

Faith Hill

Piece of My Heart

James L. Dickerson

St. Martin's Griffin ✹ New York

www.stmartins.com

Library of Congress Cataloging-in-Publication Data

Dickerson, James.
  Faith Hill : piece of my heart / James L. Dickerson.
    p. cm.
  Includes bibliographical references and discography.
  ISBN 0-312-28195-1
  1. Hill, Faith, 1967– 2. Country musicians—United States—Biography. I. Title.

  ML420.H426 D53 2001
  782.421642'092—dc21
  [B]

2001020250

First Edition: June 2001

10 9 8 7 6 5 4 3 2 1

To Janet Young and
her daughter, Marcie

Contents

Acknowledgments

I would like to thank the following people for their help with this book: Charlie Butts, Sidney Wheatley, Jennifer Byrd, Jackie Granberry, photographer Alan Mayor, Sheriff Patrick Gallivan, Robin Byrd; Kathy Lavelle at Archive Photos, John Few and the *Smith County Reformer*; Alanna Nash, music journalist extraordinaire; my literary agent for this book, Lori Perkins; and Christina Prestia, my editor at St. Martin's Press.

Faith Hill

Introduction

Faith Hill is the latest in a long line of gifted, A-list performers from Mississippi, beginning with Robert Johnson, Muddy Waters, and B. B. King, then extending through Elvis Presley, Tammy Wynette, Charley Pride, and Marty Stuart. In recent years Brandy, LeAnn Rimes, and Faith Hill have rounded out the list, taking it into the new millennium.

As a Mississippi-born writer, I am always alert to new talent emerging from the Magnolia State, especially in the areas of writing and music. That's because Mississippians defined a huge chunk of twentieth-century American pop culture, whether it was in literature—with William Faulkner, Eudora Welty, and Tennessee Williams—or in music, where innovation has been the guiding characteristic. Anyone looking for the *next big thing* would be advised to look south to Mississippi. As the music-business saying goes: Once a hit, always a threat.

For all practical purposes, Robert Johnson invented the blues, B. B. King defined electric blues, Elvis invented rock 'n' roll, Charley Pride broke the color bar, and Tammy Wynette opened the door for women to participate in country music as equal partners. When Mississippians excel in the arts, they usually carry the art to a new level, so just as a baseball scout's ears tingle when he hears the words *Cuba* or *Dominican Republic*, so do the ears of a music writer tingle when he or she hears the word *Mississippi*.

Faith Hill showed promise from the beginning, especially with the release of her hit single "Wild One." As a resident of Nashville, I was aware of the buzz surrounding her music debut, but it was difficult to assess her true potential because of the negative backlash that accompanied it. The country-music industry is distrustful of beautiful women. Attractiveness is almost always a handicap to stardom.

Faith was viewed by many on Music Row (the Nashville location where the music industry concentrates its offices) as a pretty face with little or no talent. Everyone talked about her stunning beauty. No one talked about her singing style, at least not in a positive way. From day one, she was written off as a pretender to the throne.

That might have been where the story ended, except for the fact that a revolution in music took place in 1995 and 1996. Faith became a foot soldier in that war without ever volunteering. In 1996, for the first time in history, female artists outcharted their male counterparts. Not in any year since July 1954, the year the modern music era began, had more women than men charted on the Top Twenty.

Shania Twain, who sold more than twelve million copies of her album *The Woman In Me,* played a major role, along with Alanis Morissette and Natalie Merchant, in the revolution that opened the door for women across the board. Shania was sexy, beautiful, daring in the outfits she wore, brash in her attitude, and totally dedicated to recording music that offered the female perspective on a wide range of issues. Since women purchase most of the CDs sold in America, it is not surprising that they found a voice in Shania. By the end of 2000, Shania's album sales stood at over thirty million. Soon female music fans would embrace Faith with the same enthusiasm.

As a product of the *Oprah* generation, Faith grew into womanhood convinced that her emotions were important. To Faith, finding her power as a woman was not a toss-away talk-show line, it was an intimate process that had real meaning in her own life. Her quest for stardom had more to do with finding her power as a woman than it did with dreams of seeing her name on a marquee.

Part of the joy of writing this book was discovering the real Faith Hill. Her critics and rumor mongers have painted her as manipulative, unintelligent, promiscuous, confused about her sexual identity, and lacking in talent. Her supporters see her as a talented singer whose supermodel appearance and homespun personal values make her a worthy role model. Agreeing with the latter assessment were the thousands of Internet voters in the 2000 *My VH1 Music Awards* who selected her as Woman of the Year.

With those conflicting views in mind, I decided to approach Faith's story as if it were a mystery. I wanted to find the real Faith Hill. By the time I finished researching this book, I felt I knew Faith almost as well as her mother or father.

One of several focal points in this story is Faith's adoption as an infant by a hardworking Mississippi couple, Ted and Edna Perry. The way Faith dealt with her adoption as an adult—and the intensity with which she searched for her birth mother—are critical elements of her life. It helps explain who she is and why she makes the life decisions that she does.

For that reason, I have written about her adoption in detail. I am uniquely qualified to do that. I have a degree in psychology and before becoming a writer I worked as a social worker for almost a decade. My specialty was adoption and I worked on hundreds of cases, many of them identical to Faith's situation. I have tried to use that experience to enlighten readers about what Faith faced and why resolving her identity was so important to her.

What I discovered about Faith may surprise you. I defy you to read parts of this intimate story without shedding a tear or two. I challenge you to find a more inspirational story in pop- or country-music history. Without "giving away" my discovery, I can say with confidence that Faith Hill is someone from whom we all can learn. I'm glad I took the time to get to know her, and I hope you will be, too.

CHAPTER 1

Wild One

At sixteen, Faith was still a work in progress. Tall and lanky, with pencil-thin arms and legs—and metallic braces on her teeth—she would not have drawn a second glance, except for one thing: she had the face of an angel.

On this particular day, the last Saturday in June, she and her high-school band waited patiently on the porch of a two-story log cabin at Billy John Crumpton's farm about five miles west of Raleigh, Mississippi, where she was one of the featured entertainers at a tobacco-spitting contest.

When park rangers at Bienville National Forest near Raleigh, Mississippi, egged two local residents into a tobacco-spitting competition during its annual Forestry Field Day festivities in 1952, the United States Government-sponsored contest so inflamed the competitive passions of local residents that it evolved into an annual event known as the National Tobacco Spitting contest.

Now, Faith watched as contestant after contestant sauntered out onto the makeshift stage constructed of two flatbed trucks that had been backed up perpendicular to the cabin porch. Under the rules, contestants could use the delivery method of their choice—either a two-finger pucker or an "open stance" or a between-the-teeth launch—but the chewing tobacco itself had to be approved by the judges. The goal was simply to spit the tobacco as far as possible. The world record was set by Jeff Barber in 1979 with a wad that was propelled thirty-one feet, nine-and-a-half inches.

Faith cringed after each "spit" as attendants rushed out onto the stage and wiped it clean with white towels for the next contestant. That didn't bother Faith too much since she had a grandmother who dipped snuff. She was no stranger to the sight of tobacco-pocked floors. Despite the unsightliness of the competition, it was a huge event in that part of Mississippi. There were more than three thousand people there that day, including the governor, a member of Congress, the mayor of Jackson, and the state chairman of the Republican Party. Who knew how many celebrities might be in the audience? One year, according to the Smith County Reformer, a photographer from Belgium showed up in a Yellow Cab with a New York tag.

For an aspiring singer in Mississippi, it was the equivalent of singing the National Anthem at the Super Bowl. It was the largest audience Faith had ever faced and she felt blessed to be there, representing not just her state, but the government of the United States of America. The very thought sent a patriotic flutter through her heart.

The daylong festival was broken up into several events, including weight-lifting and face-painting contests, canoe rides on a nearby pond, and a watermelon-eating free-for-all. Faith was scheduled to perform immediately after the qualifying "spits." The main event would not occur until later in the afternoon, after everyone had had an opportunity to eat their fill of barbecue.

After the final qualifying spit, someone said to Faith, "You're next." She waited until the attendant wiped the stage; then, praying she would not slip and fall on her face, she strode out onto the back of the flatbed truck, lifted her arms sweetly to the heavens and began in a cotton-soft voice what she knew to be Elvis Presley's favorite hymn:

"Amazing grace, how sweet the sound, that saved a wretch like me . . ."

Audrey Faith Perry was born on September 21, 1967, in Jackson, Mississippi, to an unwed mother who may have been as young as thirteen. Public records on the birth are sealed under court order, so little is known about Faith's natural mother, but it may be surmised that Faith's entry into the world was a source of great emotional distress for the young mother, whether she was thirteen or eighteen, or somewhere in between.

Young mothers-to-be in Mississippi have three choices: they can keep their children and raise them with the support of their parents; they can turn them over to the state department of social services for adoption placement; or they can place their children privately. It took three days for the young mother and her parents to decide what was best for them.

Ted and Edna Perry of Jackson had two sons in grammar school, Steve and Wesley, but they could have no more children of their own and they very much wanted a daughter. Or at least Edna did. Ted wasn't certain they needed another child and he had to be talked into it by his wife. He wasn't against it; he just wasn't as much in favor of raising another child as was his wife.

Perhaps fearing that Ted's lack of education would limit their chances of adoption with the state—Ted had quit school in the fourth grade so he could work and help his parents support a family of thirteen children—they asked their doctor if he knew of anyone who wanted to give up a baby girl for adoption. He said he would keep his eyes open. Ted and Edna prayed to God that a healthy baby girl would be delivered unto them.

Mississippi adoption laws are archaic at best, and barbaric at worst. The state social services agency has the responsibility of supervising adoptions of all children who have been made wards of the state. Trained social workers interview both the natural mother and prospective adoptive parents. They do home studies during which they gather social, health, and psychological information that enables them to place the child in the best available home and, at the same time, counsel the natural mother about the trauma she is undergoing. Once a child is placed in an adoptive home, the family is supervised for a specified time to make certain it is a good placement. Eventually a judge is asked to make the adoption permanent.

Private adoptions are different. In Mississippi, the procedure is similar to what someone would go through to acquire a puppy. Doctors receive requests from patients who want children and match them with other patients. All the judge wants to know is whether the natural mother has properly relinquished her rights to the child. The process is more akin to a business transaction than anything else.

Only a few days after Ted and Edna Perry contacted their doctor, they received a telephone call from him. He had a baby girl for them. She was three days old and was in good health. Ted, age thirty-seven, and Edna, age thirty-one, were ecstatic. They never expected to hear from the doctor so soon. Because their religious faith played such an important role in their decision to adopt, they chose a name that would reflect the divine grace they felt they had received from God: Audrey Faith Perry.

Actually, eight-year-old Wesley was responsible for choosing the name Audrey. Asked by Edna what they should name her, he came up with Audra, a character from his favorite television show, *The Big Valley*; mother Edna sort of smoothed it out to Audrey.

In mid-October, Ted and Edna picked up their baby girl at the doctor's office and took her home, leaving the paperwork in the hands of their lawyer. In due course the adoption was finalized and the court records sealed to public view.

For the first eleven years of her life, Faith lived in Jackson, the second-largest city on the Natchez Trace (the largest Trace city is Nashville, Tennessee). In the late 1960s and early 1970s, Jackson was a city in turmoil over school integration and the war in Vietnam.

In 1970, when Faith was three, students at Jackson State College, a predominantly black institution, took to the streets to protest the United States' invasion of Cambodia. The Jackson police responded with an armored personnel carrier loaded with men armed with Thompson submachine guns. When the smoke cleared, two students lay dead and twelve others were wounded. School buildings were riddled with bullets.

Public schools were a major issue for white parents who could not afford to send their children to private institutions. Racial prejudice played a role in that, of course, but of more concern was the issue of violence. What parent, white or black, wanted to send their children to schools where the prospect of machine-gun fire loomed as a potential threat?

But it was more than racial conflict and machine gun–toting cops that convinced Ted and Edna they needed to move to the country. The final straw was a conflict that ten-year-old Faith had with the Jackson police. Up the street from their home was a new housing development. When the new windows went up, Faith and her friends found the temptation too much to ignore. They had a rock fight and threw the stones at each other through the windows, breaking nearly every pane in the house.

"Of course, that was not a good thing," Faith explained years later to music journalist Alanna Nash. "The police were called, and my mom stopped the police before they got down there, and she said, 'You just let her have it. You do whatever you have to do to scare her to death because once she gets home, she's going to wish she'd not come home.' So we heard the police coming, and we ran really fast around the workmen's trailer, and we were hiding behind the trailer, and I was thinking, *My life's about to end right now, and I'm only ten years old.* Sure enough, the cop got us, and took us back home, and he said, 'I'm putting your name on this list. If you ever do this again, you're going to jail.' I thought, *God! Ten years old, that's pretty heavy.* And he was a big guy, and in my mind he was probably ten times larger than he really was." Telling the story, Faith laughed. "I liked to get in trouble a little bit, you know? It was kind of exciting to see how far I could go."

In 1977 Ted and Edna packed up their household possessions, along with their three children, and moved to Star, Mississippi, a tiny crossroads community located about twenty miles southeast of Jackson on Highway 49, a four-lane highway that connects Jackson with the Gulf Coast. Since the late 1950s, Ted had worked at Presto Manufacturing Company in Jackson, a plant that makes pressure cookers and other cookware. Edna worked as a bank teller. The family's relocation to Star did not affect their employment. They simply commuted to work in Jackson.

Star's population hovers around five hundred, depending on whether the death rate exceeds the birth rate in a given year. There is one street intersection, but no stoplights or stores. As small as it is, Star is cut in half by a railroad track and Highway 49, both of which basically run north to south through the community. On one side of that divide are the Star Baptist Church and the volunteer fire department, along with a smattering of homes with well-manicured lawns—and on the other side are the town's two schools and an assortment of house trailers and wooden-frame homes. Going east to west—and separating the elementary and high schools—is a highway that had a profound effect on the life of Audrey Faith Perry: local residents call it Star Road.

Ted and Edna found what they were looking for in Star. There was no big-city traffic, no racial strife, no protesters, no machine-gun fire, and, perhaps best of all, no rush to get anywhere fast. They found a place where they could raise their children to be God-fearing, hardworking Christian Americans who would grow up strong and respectful of authority. There is no Andy Griffith in Star, but there are plenty of similarities to the mythical television town of Mayberry, North Carolina.

By the time the Perry family moved to Star, Faith already knew she was adopted. In later years she would say she could not remember a time when she did not know she was adopted. Ted and Edna told Faith that her mother had become pregnant by a married man and had had no choice but to give her up for adoption. That was not true, but it was the best story they could come up with and they stuck to it.

Almost from the beginning, it was apparent that Faith had come from different stock. She started singing at age three, and where that came from no one could understand. Her first songs were church hymns, the songs she heard her mother sing around the house, the songs she later heard *everyone* sing in the Star Baptist Church.

Faith was always full of surprises. No sooner did she begin singing in front of her family members, than she started holding a hairbrush up to her face, pretending it was a microphone. She skipped from room to room, hairbrush in hand, singing the songs of her favorite entertainer, fellow Mississippian Elvis Presley. *"Don't be cruel to a heart that's true . . ."* Soon Ted and Edna were supplying their little wonder with the King's best material. Having a little Elvis in the household was entertaining, to say the least.

In May 1975, when she was seven, she pleaded with her parents to let her go to the Mississippi Coliseum to see Elvis perform in concert. Her mother refused, saying she didn't want her daughter exposed to the evils of rock 'n' roll. Faith was shocked by the turnabout. Finally a neighbor talked Edna into allowing Faith to go to the concert. Faith was blown away by the energy of it all, the pageantry of Elvis at his Las Vegas–style best. Faith knew then she wanted to be a star—just like Elvis.

But after the Perry family moved to Star, Faith started undergoing changes in her life. Before the relocation, she had not been shy about stepping center stage into the living room to perform in front of her family. Now she felt embarrassed to do that. She did most of her "performing" in her bedroom with the door closed.

Typically, she would come home from school, her actress's face displaying mock pain. Seeing the look of distress, Edna would ask, "What's the matter, honey?"

"Oh, something terrible happened today," Faith said, drooping her lower lip. "I don't want to talk about it."

With that, she would make a dramatic dash for her bedroom and close the door behind her. Safe at last, she turned on her record player—the volume turned low so her mother could not hear—and with her white hairbrush in hand she stood before the mirror and sang along to the music of Elvis, Reba McEntire, and Tammy Wynette. She swayed, dipped, spun around, and held her arms out to the adoring imaginary crowd that loved her unconditionally.

Faith's mother and father had well-defined roles in her life. Ted could not read, so he was of no help with her homework, but he was strong and honest and very protective of his only daughter. More than once he gave her permission to do something on the condition that she not tell her mother. Edna was the disciplinarian of the family, the practical one who often chastised Faith for being lazy about her chores. If Faith protested about a certain chore, Edna responded with, "Honey, you don't know what hard work is." There was nothing cruel about Edna's firm hand. She didn't do it out of meanness. She did it to protect Faith from dangers she could sense but not articulate. It was maternal instinct in its rawest, most inexplicable form.

It was during her preteen years that Faith developed what she later described as "that little mystery inside of me." She fantasized about being special. Were her biological parents of British royalty? Were they music superstars? Were they going to return to Mississippi and claim her as their own and take her away to some mansion on a hill? Perhaps her true father was none other than Elvis himself. Stranger things had happened, she knew that for a fact. Just look at all the strange things in the Bible that she heard about every Sunday in the Star Baptist Church.

That "little "mystery" inside of her gave her inspiration, offered her hope and encouragement, but it also had a flip side that sometimes nudged her into dangerous situations. From her childhood right up to the present, there have been dueling personalities inside Faith. One speaks and sings with the voice of an angel. The other speaks with the bravado of the risk-taker and the daredevil.

During her preteen years, one of the things that Faith enjoyed doing with her girlfriends was playing "chicken" with the fast freight train that sped through Star three times a day on its way to and from Jackson. Star was only a crossroads, so the train never slowed the way it would if it were going through a town. Instead, it warned residents with a shrill, ear-piercing whistle that was sometimes forceful enough to rattle windowpanes.

Faith was not afraid of the whistle—or the train. She was drawn to it the same way she was drawn to the music of Elvis Presley. For fun, Faith and one of her friends, usually Gay Knight, walked together down the center of the tracks, side by side, their girlish shoulders nearly touching. First they saw the light, the bright beacon that advanced ahead of the engine, shimmering in the distance. Then came the whistle, the loudest, most daring force to ever exist in Star. It was music to Faith's ears. Then came the overpowering sound of the train itself, a noise so loud it made the ground beneath her feet tremble with urgency. The last girl to leap from the path of the train was the bravest. As you might expect, Faith was usually the last to leap.

Ever since they had moved to Star, Faith had had a secret pact with her father. She promised to do her best to stay out of trouble, and if she felt tempted to get in trouble, she would try not to get caught by the police. For his part, he promised that if she brought her problems to him instead of her mother, he would not tell Edna about her mischief. Ted wasn't encouraging Faith to be duplicitous with her mother for any sinister reasons; his motivation was to protect Edna from the anguish she always felt over Faith's mischievous adventures. Besides, there should be some things that are only between a father and his daughter.

Faith kept that pact with her father, but there were plenty of times when she was sorely tempted to bypass it, especially when puberty came along. It hit Faith with all the awesome power of that freight train she was so fond of dueling. She did things that made no sense, things without rhyme or reason. Once she grabbed up an armful of toilet paper rolls from her own bathroom and dashed out into the night on a mission that she, least of all, understood. Her target was the home of her English teacher, a woman she admired and respected.

Silently she made her way through the shrubbery, where she remained long enough to make sure no one was around. Then, in a burst of energy that was probably as awkward as it was intense, she proceeded to roll her teacher's lawn with the toilet paper. Since she was never busted—who would ever consider sweet Faith a suspect?—she eventually moved on to her second target, the home of the music director of the Star Baptist Church. *Faith, what got into you, girl!* To this day, neither the teacher nor the music director has any idea that Faith was the culprit.

On another occasion, Faith stole a candy bar. She didn't steal it out of necessity, since her dad would have given her the money. She stole for the thrill of it. Along with the "little mystery" inside her, thrill-seeking was part of her secret life.

⌐ Star's high school and elementary school are named McLaurin Attendance Center. The only way to get there is on Star Road, a two-lane blacktop highway that connects the community with the larger town of Brandon. The school itself is set back off the road about 150 yards. It is a modern, brick structure that is much larger than it appears from the road. It is identical to most of the other schools in Mississippi, with one major exception: Most schools position the athletic fields at the rear of the school where they are not so obvious from the entrance. The layout of McLaurin Attendance Center is just the opposite.

To reach the school you must navigate an athletic gauntlet on a narrow road that runs between the football field on the left and the baseball field on the right. Clearly sports are held in high esteem at the school; indeed, sports are held in high esteem throughout the entire community. Outside of the church, it is the only unifying identity possessed by the community.

When Faith crossed the road from the elementary school to the high school, she was no great beauty. Her tall, gangly body had clearly run amok with hormones. Her legs looked like stilts; her teeth were covered with braces and her curly, mousy brown hair was hard to manage in any style except short. Childhood friends told *People* magazine that Faith was "brutally hard on herself. She was always paranoid about her body, about being lanky and tall with not very big breasts and long arms."

On the inside, she was Elvis Presley. On the outside, she was nowhere near a superstar. Despite her self-identity concerns, Faith proceeded through high school motivated by her dreams of stardom. Her mental toughness, her willingness to not accept no for an answer to her dreams, began at an early age and motivated her throughout high school. It is her most admirable quality.

By her freshman year, she was at her present adult height—five feet eight inches—and within two years she was literally the most popular girl at McLaurin Attendance Center. Her body filled out in all the right places, her hair was transformed, as if by magic, and her radiant face reflected the mystery of the superstar—she had blossomed into everyone's sweetheart. Midway through high school she was clearly Star's brightest light.

"She was so popular," recalls Adrienne Massey Cooley, who was four years younger than Faith. "She was always my idol. We cheered together. She cheered in high school and I cheered in junior high. She was homecoming queen, most popular, friendliest. Everybody wanted to be her boyfriend, all the guys."

Coach Charlie Butts taught Faith in his seventh-grade social studies class, then again in his tenth-grade social studies class. "Faith was one of those few individuals that it didn't matter what she wore, she was automatically pretty," Butts said in an interview. "I never noticed her being self-conscious [about her height]. She never hunkered over or anything. She always carried herself well."

Coach Butts was so impressed with Faith that he asked her if she would like to be the scorekeeper for the baseball team. He always chose girls for scorekeepers because they were always "a little bit smarter." For a tenth-grader like Faith, it was a dream job. Being a cheerleader was nice, but that didn't make her one of the guys. Being a scorekeeper was different. She would be one of *them*. She didn't have to think about it. She said yes immediately.

"I hand-pick my scorekeepers," says Butts. "I'll watch them in the classroom and hallways and I'll study them. A good manager and a good scorekeeper are as important as a top-notch player. I knew she would bond well with the team. It wasn't just because of her looks. I could see that she was well liked."

Coach Butts offered only one stipulation: He had a rule against the scorekeepers dating the players, and if that were to happen she would have to relinquish her job. Faith said that was fine with her. She had no intention of dating any of the players.

The no-dating rule was not unreasonable. The scorekeeper sat in the dugout with the players, rode on the bus with the players to out-of-town games (making her the only female on the bus), and was treated like one of the guys. If a scorekeeper paired off romantically with a player, it would be upsetting and distracting to the entire team.

Of course Faith did what she always did, though to be fair it must be said she never did these things intentionally. She broke the rule and fell in love with the pitcher. His name was Sidney Wheatley and he was not just the star pitcher, he was also the star quarterback for the football team. He was every high-school girl's dream.

Sidney was Faith's first serious boyfriend. They tried to keep their relationship secret, especially from Coach Butts—for the good of the team, of course—but it was difficult because they were as much in love as two high-school students could be. "It was tough in class," Wheatley told the author in an interview. "I was right there next to her and it was hard to concentrate. I think my math teacher probably got onto us a good bit for talking and tapping on shoulders and passing notes back and forth."

Winning Faith's heart was no overnight undertaking, though she probably thought it was. Recalls Wheatley: "I started school there in the eighth grade and noticed her right off the bat, but I was so shy then I wouldn't talk to any of the girls. I talked to her a little bit in the ninth grade and we were friends. It was probably through baseball and because in football she was a cheerleader and I was the quarterback. It was that sort of thing. We were always around each other, even out of school. It just seemed like the natural thing to do. Of course, I always thought she was pretty cute, too. It just took awhile to get up the guts to talk to her."

Soon the romance was obvious to everyone, including Coach Butts. "They fell madly in love and couldn't think of anything except each other," says Butts. "I told Faith, 'Look, since you've started dating—and I have no problem with that—but you'll have to stop being my scorekeeper.'" Faith didn't argue with him. She had no defense. She was in love with Sidney and she couldn't deny that. As it happened, the day that Coach found out about the romance, they had a game and Faith's services as scorekeeper were needed.

Butts suggested she sit outside the dugout. "I thought that would solve the problem," says Butts. "I probably did the worst thing I could do because she went out and sat right behind the home plate behind the fence. Sidney couldn't get the ball over the plate to save his soul. I kept thinking, *What in the world is happening here?* I was scratching my head because he had no control of the ball. For some reason I happened to glance over and see Faith sitting right behind the home plate. Instead of looking at the catcher, he was sort of veering over and looking at Faith. He was just all over the plate. Finally, I had to move her out of his line of sight, and that ended her career as scorekeeper."

Wheatley remembers being distracted that day, but doesn't recall Coach Butts being upset about it, a clear sign that he *was* distracted. "I was disappointed that she would no longer be in the dugout, but she still came to most of the games." Wheatley laughs thinking about it years later. "She was close by, but maybe not as close as I wanted her to be."

Coach Butts regretted having to kick her off the team. "Faith was always such a pleasant girl—very easy to talk to, very willing to talk to anybody," he says. "I don't guess she would mind me saying this, but she was just spacey enough to where you could pick with her and joke and carry on. She was very gullible and naive. You could tell Faith, 'We are having a nuclear attack this morning'—and she would say, 'Where do we hide?' She wasn't necessarily an outstanding student, by any stretch of the imagination, but she knew what she wanted to do. The [school] books were what she had to go through to achieve her artistic goals."

Music continued to be the focus of Faith's nonromantic moments throughout high school. She sang for anyone who wanted to listen—the school, church, business luncheons, wherever she could find an audience.

Schoolmate Terry Moody, who was two classes behind Faith, told the author that she recalls Faith singing Elvis's version of "Dixie," the National Anthem, and "Amazing Grace" at school functions. Says Moody: "She just said one day she wanted to become a singer and she did. She was always very determined."

Robin Byrd and her husband, David, helped supervise the church youth ensemble. They often drove them to other churches in the area, where they sang for the various congregations. On one such trip, David asked the youngsters what they wanted to be when they grew up. "I know what I'm going to be," answered Faith, who was in the ninth grade. "I'm going to be a country singer." Robin, who today works in the principal's office, said she wasn't surprised by Faith's comment. "We had no doubt that she would do it."

In some respects, Faith was like those children who are pushed into beauty pageants at an early age by obsessive parents, except in Faith's case it was not her mother who pushed her into competition; Faith pushed herself. She was a cheerleader, baseball scorekeeper, a member of the student council, and each year when the students voted for their class favorite and most beautiful, it was always Faith who walked away with the most votes.

In Mississippi, the highest honor that an adolescent girl can achieve is being voted homecoming queen. There are those who feel that Faith was the most radiant homecoming queen ever to represent the McLaurin Tigers football team.

Despite the honors, Faith was unhappy. As early as thirteen and fourteen, she told friends that she was suffocating in Star and needed to find a way to escape. "This is a dreadful place," she told one friend. "I've got to find a way to get out quick. I can't wait until I'm eighteen or nineteen."

Faith's salvation was music. Somehow she knew she had to find a way to release the Little Elvis that lived inside of her. The older she got, the more her mother urged her to focus on her goals. "My mother hated [the cheerleading]," Faith told Alanna Nash. " 'You want to be a singer!' " Faith said, mimicking her mother. " 'I'm telling you, it's going to ruin your voice. All you do is get out there and yell and scream and holler in those short skirts.' "

Coach Charlie Butts was aware of Faith's musical talents, but he recalls only one occasion that he actually heard her sing. Faith tipped him off in advance that she and a friend would be performing in an assembly program.

"She knew I was a big Alabama fan and she told me that they were going to sing an old Alabama song," he recalled. "She had a guy playing the piano and she and her friend sang the song. That was the first time I realized that she had an ability to harmonize. You knew she had a good voice, but you think, *Oh, that's good, she'll do well at church*, but you never dream they will be famous. . . . You knew if looks had anything to do with it, she would make it.

"In today's entertainment business, if you can combine appearance with talent, you have a pretty good shot of making it. She is probably one of the most beautiful women in the world—and she's getting prettier every year. I was standing in line at the Jitney-Jungle [a Southern supermarket chain]. I looked up and there was Faith, about seven feet tall in this Pepsi poster. It was kind of a funny feeling."

Just about the only person Faith didn't discuss her music ambitions with was her high-school sweetheart Sidney Wheatley. "That was probably because she knew I wasn't all that musically inclined," he says with a laugh. When they were together, she usually deferred to his choice for a radio station, but that worked out fine because they were both interested in the same type of country and pop music. "She had her favorites like Reba and George Strait, people that she really enjoyed," he said in an interview. "Now I think about how ironic that is. Now she's right up there alongside them."

There weren't many opportunities for teens in Star, especially those who had paired off in romantic relationships. "There was nothing really close by," says Wheatley. "If Faith and I didn't go to Jackson, which is where you would go to the movies or to get something to eat, sometimes we would go to Ridgeland [a Jackson suburb] to get something to eat. Other times we would just go over to each other's house and watch movies."

Neither of their parents were too happy about their relationship. The concern was that they would get too "serious" and end up another teenage marriage statistic. Certainly Ted and Edna Perry didn't want Faith to become either a married teen or an unmarried mother. Ted left the counseling to Edna. His advice to Faith was the same as it always had been: "Do whatever you want to do, but don't let your mother find out."

"I got in trouble for staying on the phone at night too late, getting phone calls past nine o'clock in high school," Faith told Alanna Nash. "I would always be the one to get in trouble. I could never figure it out. I thought, *Well, they're calling me. You know, I didn't call them!*"

After Sidney and Faith had dated for two years, his parents figured it had gone far enough. They had nothing against Faith or her family. They were fearful of Faith getting pregnant and ruining their son's future. Faith was a beautiful girl, but no one expected her to ever be anything other than that. By contract, Sidney was the school's star quarterback and pitcher. Everyone expected him to be the real star of McLaurin Attendance Center. It was not an unrealistic expectation. Coach Butts had sent another pitcher off to college and then on to the Baltimore Orioles. Everyone, including Coach Butts, figured that Sidney had a real future as a professional baseball player.

At the end of his junior year Sidney's parents requested that he break up with Faith. They loved Faith, but they loved him more and they did not want to see him throw away his future. Faith was a dreamer, but he was headed for the big leagues. Reluctantly, Sidney agreed to do as his parents asked.

Interviewed in 2000, Sidney remembers the breakup as if it were yesterday. "It was awful," he says. "I was late for school and I had to go into class [after it had begun]. I was all upset." Faith sat behind him in class and she could see that he was upset. She tapped him on the shoulder and tried to talk to him. He said he didn't want to talk about it and, of course, that only made her more determined to find out what was wrong. Finally he told her, whispered to her right there in class that they would have to break up.

"I was all upset about it and I couldn't hardly talk, and she was tapping me on the shoulder," he says. "And finally the teacher lets us go out into the hallway." There in the hallway of McLaurin Attendance Center Sidney broke up with a girl who would someday be known as one of the world's most successful and beautiful women. "It was devastating," he says. "I was seventeen and she was my first serious girlfriend."

Today, nearly a decade and a half after that breakup, Sidney is happily married and has children. Now a popular baseball coach in a small community not far from Jackson, he never made it into the pros, choosing instead to serve a four-year stint with the United States Air Force.

When he returned to Mississippi, Faith was a country-music superstar. "I'm thrilled for her," he says. Her success surprised him, but not because he thought she didn't have the talent to succeed in Nashville. "I just figured, like most people, that so much goes into something like that, like timing. I never had any doubts she could do it, but the odds are so great. Faith was always a special person to me and to anyone who was around her."

The breakup hit Faith hard, too. It was her first serious relationship also, and its termination had seemingly come from nowhere. It made her even more determined to escape the confining smallness of Star. After watching her drag her wounded psyche around town all summer, her friends decided to do something special for her eighteenth birthday in September. They held a big surprise party for her at the home of one of her classmates. They had done everything they could think of to help Faith get over her breakup with Sidney, but nothing seemed to work.

What Faith needed was an encounter with another man. For that, they went to the yellow pages of the Jackson telephone directory. They decided to hire a male stripper to perform for her at her birthday party, says schoolmate Terry Moody. That would certainly perk her up.

Unfortunately, the stripper was a no-show. "We were all glad," says Moody. "Our parents would have killed us."

⌐ Star, Mississippi, was not so entertainment-poor that it did not have a secret place where teenagers could congregate, socialize, and make out in their cars and trucks. They called it the sandpits. Actually it was a gravel quarry. The sand was left in place after the big machinery scooped up the gravel. The sandpits were as barren and otherworldly as any moonscape, but when you live in a small town you tend to gather at any location that looks different from everything else.

Like everyone else her age, Faith hung out at the sandpits with her friends during her senior year of high school, though she was careful not to fall into another serious relationship that could leave her with a broken heart. Her last year of high school was like all the other years, filled with honors and awards. The thing that was different about Faith that year was the increased effort she put into her music. She sang her heart out for any individual, congregation, or organization that would listen.

On the outside, Faith was unchanged. She was still the happy girl with the ready smile and the pleasing personality. It was on the inside that her world was in chaos. She had been rejected by her boyfriend, the love of her young life. She had been rejected by her birth mother, for reasons unknown. She loved her adoptive parents and brothers, but she was different from them, and that, itself, was a form of rejection. Worst of all, she had a Little Elvis inside of her that was kicking and screaming to get out.

After high-school graduation in May 1986, Faith and her forty-seven-member class went to the Mississippi Gulf Coast for one last fling together. It was a rite of passage that has existed for as long as the state has had public schools. The Gulf Coast has everything a graduating senior could want to complete that passage—nightclubs, strip joints, sand and sun, and the privacy of hotel rooms in which hold-out virgins can give it up before going out into the world as adults.

When Faith returned to Star after the class party, Ted and Edna wanted to know what her plans were. Some of her classmates were going on to college, others planned on marriage or establishing careers. Faith said she wanted to be a singer. *Yes, but what are you going to do besides that?* asked her parents. Beyond finding a way to give the Little Elvis inside of her his freedom, Faith had no idea what she was going to do.

As the summer of 1986 wore on, it became apparent that Faith would have to do something. She couldn't just sit around the Perry household, pretending to be a singer. She was Star's homecoming queen, for heaven's sake. She had responsibilities to the community. Finally her brothers, Steve and Wesley, talked her into enrolling in Hinds Community College, a two-year institution that had a branch campus in Raymond, only about a thirty-minute drive from Star. Faith could live at home and pursue her singing and get educated at the same time. It was the perfect compromise.

Hinds Community College is one of the oldest institutions of its type in the nation. It began in 1917 as an agricultural high school, but by 1922 it was offering college-level courses. For years, it was part of Mississippi's junior college system. By the time Faith entered in the fall of 1986, the degrading "junior" identification had been dropped, replaced by the more dignified "community college" designation. Typically it enrolls ten to twelve thousand students a semester.

Faith jumped into her schoolwork with a passion. She wasn't terribly excited about going to school, but she wanted to please her parents and brothers. She applied for a position on the popular recruiting team named the Hinds Connection and was one of only twenty-five students chosen.

"It's very selective," explains Jackie Granberry, who today supervises the Hinds Connection. "We go through a procedure that includes several interviews and some training. They serve the college as official hosts and they go out to the schools to recruit students."

Faith also obtained a job working in the school development office, which supervises the Hinds Connection. "Faith was just as cute and bubbly as she could be," said Granberry. "She had short hair then and was full of life. The main thing I remember about her was that never, ever, did I see her not smiling or down. She was so peppy and was always singing. She just sang all the time, just humming and singing."

Faith's boss in the Office of Development was Bill Buckner, who also served as the school's head football coach. Perhaps because he had two daughters of his own, he took a special interest in Faith. "She was a real bright person, you know," he said. "I always tried to help her out." One day Faith confided in Buckner about her need to find her natural mother. "I told her I would love to help her," he says. "The people that took her in, she loved them and did not want to hurt them, but inside she had this yearning to know."

Faith was a very enthusiastic member of the Hinds Connection and was always ready to sing for any group selected by the school. "She had a servant's heart and was a very likable person," said Buckner. Once he asked her to sing for the Fellowship of Christian Athletes. She showed up with her own tape and proceeded to sing the Baptist hymns she had learned in Star. "We had about sixty or seventy athletes and they were really blessed by [her singing]," he says. "She was a special person that the Lord had created. I think that was the thing that made her enjoyable to be around."

As a representative of the school, Faith also sang for prisoners at the Hinds County Jail, which was located near the school. "I'd go in and sing 'Amazing Grace,' and sometimes read a Bible verse or something, or give a testimony, just talk about what I was doing in school, and something that happened in my life that really was exciting or something," Faith told Alanna Nash. "It was like [being] Santa Claus. Like when you see a child who sees Santa Claus at a mall. These prisoners just . . . It breaks my heart, you know. I believe in justice, and I think if you break the law, especially murderers, or kidnappers or rapists, you belong in prison, period. But it's really sad."

The students in Hinds Connection were a close-knit group, according to Granberry, who says that the boys and girls in the group tended to "hang out together." Once a group of them went squirrel hunting. Does it surprise her that Faith would go into the woods on a squirrel-hunting expedition? Not really, she says. "A lot of good ole country boys live around Raymond, and I can imagine them all saying, 'Let's go squirrel hunting this afternoon,' and girls like Faith who had never been squirrel hunting would say, 'Yes, let's do it.'" Faith had lots of friends in the Connection, male and female, but Granberry says she never saw her pair off with one of the male students. "I don't remember her having a boyfriend."

One day near the end of the semester Faith shocked Granberry and Buckner by announcing that she was going to drop out of school to pursue her singing career. "I remember the day she came in to tell us that she was not coming back," says Granberry. "Now was the time she needed to go and do her thing. We did everything possible to talk her into coming back to school. You need an education. If [the singing] doesn't work out, you'll need to have a skill to fall back on."

But Faith was adamant about leaving. She had thought about it and prayed about it, and she just knew in her heart that she was not cut out for school. "Bill [Buckner] talked to her," says Granberry. "He had children her same age. He talked to her like a daddy would talk to her. I can remember Bill saying, 'I would like for you to stay here. You've got time to go off to Nashville.' "

When school broke for the Christmas holidays, Granberry and Buckner were hopeful they would see her again when the second semester began in January 1987. That didn't happen. They never saw her again.

Years later, when Faith became famous, Granberry and Buckner were jubilant. "I never dreamed she would do what she has done, but I knew she was gifted," says Buckner. "Today, if we ever hear that she is going to be on television, we always tune in. I am a fan of country music, mainly because of her."

Granberry laughs about their attempts to keep Faith in school. "That doesn't speak too highly of us, but when she told us that she was going to be a singing star one day, we were all like that line between reality and not upsetting her goals," she says with a laugh. "We'd say, 'Oh sure, right . . . ' All of us who are still here have laughed many times. See how much we knew!"

CHAPTER 2

Let Me Let Go

Faith pulled out of Hinds Community College before she had a plan firmly in place. She told Ted and Edna that she wanted to move to Nashville to become a country-music star. They discouraged her, perhaps pointing out that she had never left tiny Star except for trips to Jackson and the Gulf Coast. Ted and Edna had moved to Star to protect their children. Now their daughter wanted to move to a city that was twice as large as Jackson. Didn't she know that it was a tough, unforgiving world out there?

Faith was now obsessed with becoming a country-music star, but it wasn't her only obsession. Her yearning to know more about her birth mother escalated when she dropped out of college. Faith's obsession with finding her birth mother is not unusual, especially among adopted children who are very creative. Being gifted in the arts, they invariably want to understand the source of their talent. But although her parents were sympathetic and supportive, they didn't feel it was their place to track down a woman who had asked for anonymity eighteen years ago.

Laws are written to protect the identities of unwed mothers for good reason: many are minors who have become pregnant through incest, rape, and assorted other horrors. In their wisdom, judges and lawmakers have agreed that protecting unwed mothers is of equal importance to protecting their children. Often, both *are* children.

Edna must have felt besieged during the early months of 1987. Her only daughter had dropped out of school and was obsessing over finding her birth mother and moving to Nashville. For a mother who had devoted her life to protecting her children, it must have been a very emotional time. Probably for that reason, Ted stepped in and resolved the situation the only way he knew how. He told Faith that he thought moving to Nashville was a mistake, but he would help her do that if she was certain that was what she really wanted. Faith was certain.

In March 1987, Ted recruited the help of a neighbor who owned a pickup truck and, together with another neighbor's help, they loaded Faith's meager possessions into the back of the truck. Edna told Faith that she was naive to believe in such a storybook dream, and of course Mother was right: Only a hopelessly naive person would attempt to do the impossible. The odds of Faith finding success in Nashville as a country singer were astronomical.

With Faith and the two neighbors sitting in the cab of the truck—and Ted sitting in the back—they set out for Nashville on the Natchez Trace, a two-lane federal highway that has a posted speed limit of fifty miles per hour. It would be an eight-hour trip through some of the most desolate countryside in Mississippi, Alabama, and Tennessee. You can drive for hours on the Trace without ever seeing another person or automobile.

In a strange sort of way the journey made sense, as if it were part of some ancient mythical ritual that had to be observed without anyone ever knowing why. The first large town they passed through was Kosciusko. It was the hometown of Oprah Winfrey; a Mississippian who had beaten the odds. At the midway point, two hundred miles from Jackson, was Tupelo, Mississippi, the hometown of Elvis Presley and Tammy Wynette, both of whom had been naive enough to think they could beat the odds.

None of that occurred to Ted Perry, who made the entire eight-hour journey sitting in a cardboard box as the chilly March winds whipped across the bed of the truck like baby cyclones. There was no radio, no conversation with the other passengers. He must have been the loneliest man in Mississippi. He was taking his only daughter to a city that had a reputation for grinding up young girls like raw meat. The only thing this proud Mississippian, who couldn't read a book for inspiration or write a letter for self-therapy, had to cling to was his deep, abiding faith in his daughter. He didn't much believe in Nashville, but he believed in Faith with all his heart.

In the late 1980s, Nashville was a city in transition—socially, economically, and musically. At its best, it was better than anything Ted could have imagined. At its worst, it was grittier than any nightmare Ted could have experienced. Mississippi had its share of moonshine, illegal drugs, and prostitutes, but they were kept out of sight. Nashville was different. The largest ads in the yellow pages of the telephone book were for escort services, many of which were fronts for young, starry-eyed prostitutes, some of whom had turned to the life after seeing their dreams of musical stardom dashed.

Strip joints populated the downtown area and illegal drugs were available on nearly every street corner. One of the most famous "lap-dancing" establishments in the South is located just around the corner from Music Row, the heart of the city's music district.

Musically, Nashville was on the verge of something big. After the "urban cowboy" craze and the "outlaw" adventure had run their courses, country music was left to simmer with the music of Alabama, Reba McEntire, and the Highwaymen (Johnny Cash, Waylon Jennings, Willie Nelson, and Kris Kristofferson). Beginning in the mid-1980s, record-company executives started looking for a new direction. By the late 1980s, Capitol Records had signed a pudgy, bright-eyed Oklahoma marketing major named Garth Brooks. RCA Records signed the former lead singer of the country-rock band Pure Prairie League, Vince Gill. MCA Records signed a music refugee from Kentucky, Patty Loveless. CBS Records (now Sony) signed Marty Stuart, the Sweethearts of the Rodeo, and Mary Chapin Carpenter. And so it went for the remainder of the decade.

Two of the most successful and respected label heads of that era were RCA Records chief Joe Galante and Rick Blackburn, president of CBS Records' Nashville office. "There's a clear signal coming back from the marketplace, from the fans, that simply says, 'I like country music as well as I did five years ago, but give me something new, fresh and exciting,' " said Blackburn in 1987. "That's a clear signal. If you ignore the signal, you will have serious problems. The fan base is now responding to a sound first and the artist second. . . . The new artists who are coming in, they are the ones we are having success with. It's an exciting time right now to be in country music, but you're happy on one hand and you're saddened on the other because there is a displacement process. The newer ones are displacing the seasoned veterans."

Also sensing major shifts in the country-music industry was Joe Galante. "One of the things [RCA] always has been is an innovator, and I see that continuing, whether it is done through music or through the way we take music to the marketplace," said Galante in 1988. "The one thing I see happening over the next few years is that country music is going to become an exportable commodity again, which it hasn't been over the past several years." What RCA and CBS needed, indeed what all the record labels needed, were new artists who could have worldwide appeal. They would leave no stone unturned.

When Faith Perry rode into Nashville in a pickup truck, she headed straight into a tornado not unlike the one that transported the fictional Dorothy to the land of Oz. Of course, Faith was clueless about what lay in store for her. She had never heard of Rick Blackburn, Joe Galante, or Martha Sharp, an acquisitions executive at Warner Brothers.

Before leaving Star, Faith had talked to a Nashville-based gospel singer, Kenny Henson. She had shared the spotlight with him at one of the church-sponsored events she did in Mississippi. He told her that if she was going to move to Nashville she should go to the outskirts where it was "cheaper and safer."

Faith chose Hendersonville, a suburb located northeast of Nashville. She may or may not have known that Hendersonville is the home of the great Johnny Cash. It is a sprawling community with no ghettos or skyscrapers; it resembles the "safe" communities that surround Jackson, outposts of civility and sameness. With Ted's help, she located an apartment that she could afford (she had saved some money for just this eventuality) and she settled into her new home.

"I was so naive, in every way possible," Faith told *US Weekly* in a 2000 interview. "My mother said, 'You're way too trusting.' But they realized this was my dream. [My parents] just had to pray they'd given me a solid backbone, and they knew if I wanted to come home, I could."

One can only imagine what was going through Ted's mind as he made the long drive back to Star. He must have been terrified by the thought of leaving his eighteen-year-old princess all alone in a city that he knew had a dark side to it. But on the other hand he must have been terribly proud of Faith for taking on the challenge. Moving to Nashville from Star was comparable to moving to a foreign country. It required a brave heart to start a new life in a foreign land, without money, friends, or immediate prospects.

Faith wasted no time looking for work. Most of the music-related businesses and companies are located on Music Row, a parallel set of streets not far from downtown. CBS Records, RCA Records, Capitol, MCA Records, Warner Brothers Records—all were located on Music Row, with dozens of music publishers, sound companies, public-relations firms, and managers' offices located in the buildings that surrounded the major labels. That was in 1988. Since then Capitol changed its name to Liberty and moved to another part of town (and then changed its name back to Capitol). So has MCA. But in 1998, all the buildings that Faith considered essential to the realization of her dreams were laid out like ducks in a row.

Faith literally went door-to-door in her search for a job. She hoped to find a job answering phones, doing secretarial work, addressing envelopes, doing anything that would pay her bills and keep her in close contact with the movers and shakers of the music industry. "Hi, my name is Faith Perry," she said, flashing her homecoming-queen smile. She explained that she was looking for work and was willing to do anything to help out around the office. Sometimes she made it past the receptionists. Most times she never got past the front door. If she were lucky enough to get an interview, the first question was always the same: "So you're here from Mississippi. Are you a singer?"

Faith answered truthfully. Yes, she was a singer who had dreamed her entire life of making it big in Nashville. It was at that point she was usually shown to the door. What Faith didn't understand is that people who have made it in the music business don't surround themselves with people who have ambitions of stardom. That's not what they look for when they hire people to answer their telephones or type their letters. They want the best receptionist or typist they can hire, someone who will not be distracted by the glittery addiction of the music business.

Faith's honesty shot her down from job after job. She simply didn't understand how the system worked. She also failed to take into consideration the competitiveness of the receptionists she dealt with, women who were themselves aspiring recording artists.

One of the offices she almost certainly entered was MTM Records, a new label located about one block off the main drag on Music Row. The first person she would have encountered would have been the receptionist, Trisha Yearwood, an attractive blonde from a small town in Georgia who went on to become a major country-music star. But at that time she was trying her best to break into the business. "[Yearwood] was fairly self-effacing," MTM head Howard Stark told writer Lisa Rebecca Gubernick. "I guess I knew she was a singer, but she never bothered anyone with her tapes. Whatever she was doing, it seemed to be outside the office."

Realistically, how helpful would Yearwood or any other aspiring singer/ receptionist be to an eighteen-year-old drop-dead gorgeous woman who proclaimed herself a star-in-waiting? Faith didn't understand the politics of making it big in country music. How could she possibly have known?

"After I was here about two week, I just freaked out," she confided to Alanna Nash. "I said, *This is a big mistake. How in the world do I think I'm going to make it here? I don't have a job, and I hardly know anybody.*" Each day, after pounding the pavement of Music Row, Faith went home in tears. She cried her heart out. "I was really confused because I felt I'd really gotten myself in a bind. I didn't know how to deal with it. So I called my mom up, and I said, 'Mom, did I ever want to be anything else in my life, like a nurse, besides a singer?' And she said, 'Nope. This is what you've always wanted to do.' So she said, 'You need to hang up the phone and get busy, and just not worry about other things.' So I did. And I started to see myself again as a singer. It's almost as if I had to wake up in the morning and write, 'You are a singer! Don't forget that!' on the mirror with my lipstick."

In 1988 the city was filled with men and women who had dreams of stardom. Future stars such as Patty Loveless and Garth Brooks were walking the streets along with Faith. Thin and braless, Loveless looked more like a liberal-arts student than a singer. She broke out that year with the release of two albums on MCA, but early in the year she was just another one of the wannabes.

Brooks was in Nashville for the second time. His first stab at stardom had come in 1985. He drove into Nashville from Oklahoma, spent one day and night; then, running into the same resistance encountered by Faith, drove back home. Two years later he tried it again, only this time he was determined to beat the system.

There are lots of myths associated with making it in Nashville, but the very worst of them is this notion that you can arrive in the city, find a job singing in a nightclub, and then get "discovered" by a music mogul. The reality is that record-company executives seldom go to music venues to discover new talent. They go there to get a beer or scotch on the rocks, and maybe a good steak.

Most of the new acts are signed outside Nashville. "It's in places you wouldn't expect," says Rick Blackburn, who was head of CBS Records in 1988. "It's not all here in Nashville, I can tell you that. We are spending a fortune on rental cars, airline tickets, and hotel rooms, but we don't want to leave any rock unturned. The chances are it isn't knocking on your door in Nashville."

Garth Brooks figured that out before returning to Nashville. While Faith was walking the streets looking for a music-related job, Garth was managing a boot store near Music Row. His wife Sandy worked in the store with him, so she could take care of business and stand guard while Garth sought refuge in the back room to write songs.

Faith was surrounded by people with similar dreams, but she had no way of finding them. Lonely and depressed about her lack of success, she continued to knock on doors, hoping against hope that the next door would open up to her dreams. March, April, May, June—the months passed by like the windblown pages of calendars in old movies. Sometime during that period—most likely it was May—she met Daniel Sawyer Hill, a publishing executive at Polygram Publishing Company.

Hill had no job for her at Polygram, but he took down her telephone number in the event the situation changed. To Faith's surprise, she received a call from him. He asked her out on a date. Faith said yes. He was much older than Faith—he was thirty and she was eighteen—but he was a handsome, easygoing man who, in appearance, was not unlike the older professional men she met at Hinds Community College. He was born in Oak Ridge, Tennessee, a small city of twenty-eight thousand residents in the eastern part of the state. He had never been married and seemed well established in his career.

Faith was thrilled to be asked out by a member of the Music Row establishment. He was her first real friend in Nashville. She felt she could learn a lot from him about the business. Not surprisingly, their friendship quickly turned romantic. Soon she was involved in her first serious relationship since her breakup with Sidney Wheatley.

Fan Fair is the Super Bowl of country music. Held each June, the weeklong festival gives fans an opportunity to meet their favorite country entertainers up close and to hear them perform. The festival was begun in April 1972 in an effort to shunt autograph-hunting music fans away from the Country Music DJ Convention, where industry executives preferred to meet the stars away from the clamor of the fans.

The first Fan Fair was held in Nashville's Municipal Auditorium and attracted more than five thousand fans. By 1982 the event had become so popular that it was moved to the Tennessee State Fairgrounds, where there was room for the twenty thousand–plus fans that descended upon the city each June from all over the country.

By 1987, Fan Fair offered an irresistible marketing opportunity for country-music artists. In addition to a stage where music continued non-stop throughout the week, there were more than one hundred exhibit booths where fans could obtain autographs from their favorite stars, purchase T-shirts and novelties, and down their limit of corn dogs, Goo-Goo Clusters, and Moon Pies.

Fan Fair 1987 offered Faith Perry her first opportunity for a job. After nearly four months of searching, she was hired to work in Reba McEntire's booth. Her job title: T-shirt sales associate. It wasn't much of a job—and it only lasted one week—but for Faith it was like winning the lottery. She finally had her foot in the door of the music business.

Reba was Faith's favorite female singer. She knew the words to most of Reba's songs and the idea of working alongside her in the booth as she signed autographs was exciting beyond comprehension.

As fate would have it, 1987 was a watershed year for both Faith and Reba. Only weeks before Fan Fair, Reba had won her first Grammy. The previous year, the Country Music Association had awarded Reba its highest honor, Entertainer of the Year, and for the past several years, she had taken home top honors from both the Nashville-based CMA and the Los Angeles–based Academy of Country Music.

As Reba and Faith worked together in that booth, struggling with both the heat and the unending push of fans clamoring for autographs, something was happening in the music industry that would affect both women in a profound way. Reba thought she was at the top of her game in 1987, especially after winning a Grammy, but it was really the beginning of the end for Reba as a recording artist. She had no way of knowing it then, but later that year she would win the CMA award for Female Vocalist of the Year and it would be the last award she would receive from the organization until 1994. By 1997 she would no longer even be nominated for awards. Reba would find success as a movie actress and her concerts would continue to be big draws into the 1990s, but her career as a superstar recording artist was effectively over.

To use a phrase favored by Southerners, Reba was considered "too big for her britches." She insisted on studio involvement in the production of her recordings. She injected high-energy pop music into her stage act. She started up her own publishing company and promoted her own concerts. She bought a building across the road from the state fairgrounds, where Fan Fair was held, and she established her own management firm, Starstruck Entertainment. In effect, she took her music directly to her fans, bypassing the industry speed bumps that had been in place for years. To make matters even worse, she tended to hire only females.

For the conservative, male-dominated country-music establishment, all that was too much to bear; it showed its disapproval by ignoring her at the awards ceremonies. Faith would come to understand that system—

and later she herself would become a target of that system—but for now she was just happy to be making a few bucks hawking T-shirts for Reba. Years later, when asked about that association, Reba told *People* magazine: "Faith was a bright, spunky, feisty girl—real sweet and open, but a little mischievous. She reminded me a lot of myself. When she got nervous or a little flustered, her neck would break out in a rash."

When the job working for Reba came to an end, Faith was right back where she had started. She entered her fifth month in Nashville with no prospects of landing a full-time job. Fortunately, Ted and Edna sent her money to keep her going, but Faith was at the lowest point in her life—her music career was not progressing the way she had hoped and the Little Elvis inside of her was getting restless. The prospect of returning to Star was more than she could stand. What would she be able to do with her life in a small town like Star? She could return to Hinds Community College, but she already knew that was not the answer. She began obsessing about her natural mother even more.

The only thing Faith had going for her was her relationship with Daniel Hill. He told her he wanted to take care of her. He told her that everything would be all right. Although they only had been dating for a few weeks, Daniel asked Faith to marry him.

On July 23, 1987, little more than four months after she arrived in Nashville, Faith married Daniel Hill and moved into his home on Belmont Boulevard not far from the state fairgrounds. Faith's immediate problem was over—she no longer had to have a job to survive—but her quest to break into the music business was only just beginning.

Now that she was married, all her efforts went into furthering her career. During the day she networked and looked for an entry-level position in a music-related business. At night, she and Daniel went out on the town to listen to music.

Faith settled in for the long haul.

Somebody Stand by Me

Gary Morris was an enigma. Signed by Warner Brothers in the early 1980s, the rugged-looking Texan recorded several albums before moving on to MCA/Universal and then, later on, to Liberty Records. He was handsome, but he wore his hair long and often sported a full beard, thus putting himself at odds with the clean-shaven look preferred by Nashville record executives. Despite his Texas upbringing, his voice was devoid of twang and leaned toward the pop spectrum of the country charts. His 1984 hit, "Wind Beneath My Wings," won Song of the Year awards from both the Country Music Association and the Academy of Country Music.

By 1988 Morris had expanded his career to include acting. He co-starred on Broadway in *La Bohème* with Linda Ronstadt, and he starred in the opera *Les Misérables*, becoming the first American to play the part of Jean Valjean. He also co-starred in a television series called *The Colbys*, a spinoff of the hugely successful prime-time soap, *Dynasty*.

Nashville wasn't sure what to think about Morris. He could bring you to tears with his powerful voice, even if it did tend to sound a little too pop, but what was the deal with the beard and the long hair? He didn't look or sing anything like George Jones, that was for sure. If he was a country singer, why was he performing on Broadway? Nashville branded him an outlaw, though a very pleasant one.

Morris thought it was much ado about nothing. He got involved with *La Bohème* and *Les Misèrables* because his record label and management company had asked him to give it a try. "I didn't particularly want to at that time," Morris said. "As a matter of fact, I passed on it two or three times. Opera wasn't then—and is not now—my cup of tea. But those shows were wonderful."

Morris even saw parallels between *Les Misérables'* Jean Valjean and himself. "He was a man of great conviction and strength and determination, and I think personally I am at least a man of determination. . . . He was a man of great sensitivity, which you didn't expect in him, at least the way I portrayed him. I think there are parts of me that are carefully enclosed behind certain shields that are imminently sensitive to things that I don't let people know about, so that is probably true, too."

Faith Hill was drawn to the mystique of Gary Morris. He was more than a country singer. He was a star who was as comfortable on Broadway or on a Hollywood soundstage as he was in a Nashville juke joint or steak house. He was determined in his career, but he was protective of his secret self, the one that allowed him to toss off his cowboy hat and slip into the character of Jean Valjean. Those were qualities that Faith thought she had within herself.

After months of rejections at offices all up and down Music Row, Faith decided to apply for work at Gary Morris Productions, an office that housed the singer's publishing and production company. This time she played it smart.

"I was sitting there in that chair, and they were interviewing me, and they said, 'Are you here in Nashville to be a singer or writer?'" Faith related to Alanna Nash. "I said, 'No.' I thought, *Where in the hell did that come from? Yes, I'm here to become a singer!* But it was survival. . . . If they had asked me, 'Are you here to be in the music business,' and if I had said, 'Yeah—do you have a band? Do you know somebody?' . . . Well, that was not what they wanted to hear. So when I went to Gary's office, I said no, I was not a singer—and that was about the lowest point, that first year, because I was so confused. I was afraid, and at that point very, very naive, and I was still trying to figure it out. I mean, I had not been out of Star, Mississippi. It's a lot different here, and especially coming right in, my first job, working for an entertainer, of all people."

Faith leaped into her job with enthusiasm. Outside of the student job she had had at Hinds Community College, it was her only experience in the workplace. Her job was to answer the telephones, do typing and filing as needed, and run interference for Morris and his associates to protect them from starry-eyed singers and songwriters. That must have brought a smile to her face. Now she understood the system. All those unfriendly people who had refused to allow her past the front door, she now realized, had nothing against her or her talent—they were simply doing their job.

For the first time in a long time Faith was able to relax. She had a husband who wanted to take care of her and she had a job on Music Row. She wondered if perhaps she had overshot her ambitions. Perhaps her destiny was in the business end of the industry and not as a singer. Always eager to please, Faith was the best receptionist she could be. She did everything she was asked to do and she volunteered for jobs that were not expected of her.

Faith's tenure at Gary Morris Productions coincided with a stressful time in the entertainer's life. All entertainers feel stressed when their careers begin to atrophy, but Morris's stress was for the opposite reason— he was overworked. One positive result of the stress was a hit song, "Leave Me Lonely."

"I think when I wrote it I was doing too much," Morris explained in a 1988 radio interview. "I was doing *The Colbys*, I was running out to do concerts. I remember one particular week I shot an episode of the *The Colbys* and did a video for a song, which was like three days long. I did two or three concerts and at the end of the week I had had like twenty hours' sleep in seven days. Meanwhile, some of those people out there who call themselves fans were becoming disturbed with me. I did a couple of concerts and wouldn't sign autographs because I didn't have time. We finished at midnight, rolled onto the bus, and there was a bit of, *I don't want to see anybody*. I just wanted to be by myself, which prompted the song."

Ironically, Faith was manning the phones the day of that interview, which called for Morris to show up at a specified time at a Music Row studio where the program, *Pulsebeat—The Voice of the Heartland*, was taped. When he didn't appear on time, frantic telephone calls went back to the office. No one in his office knew where he was. He was supposed to be at the studio. As it turned out, he had had some sort of car trouble, but he was calm and collected when he arrived at the studio. Notified that her missing star had been located, Faith voiced relief and returned to her regular, noncrisis duties.

Despite Faith's devotion to her job, there was one habit she could not break: she could not stop singing. She sang around Morris's office just as she had done at Hinds Community College when she thought no one was around.

One day, when she thought she was alone in her second-floor office, she turned the radio up real loud and started singing along to the music. David Chase, one of the songwriters who worked out of Morris's office, was downstairs at the time. Hearing Faith's voice, he ran up the stairs and caught Faith in the act of singing.

"I knew it!" he said. "I knew what you were here to do!"

Faith was busted. Part of her was happy, especially since Chase said good things about her voice, but another part of her was terrified that she would now lose her job. Chase was so impressed with her voice that he asked her to sing the demo for a new song he had written, titled "It Scares Me." He promised he would not tell a soul or play the demo for anyone there in the office.

Faith agreed to do the recording. After-hours, when everyone else in the office had gone home for the day, she and Chase went downstairs to the studio and recorded the song. Faith was elated. "It Scares Me" was her first demo. For her, that was a big deal, even if it did have to be kept a secret.

Several weeks later, Gary Morris came into the office, spoke to Faith, and went downstairs to the studio. Morris was always nice to Faith, but she always felt intimidated whenever he was around. Part of it had to do with his stardom, but mostly it had to do with his size—he's a big, muscular man who chose music over football, despite a scholarship to play at the college level—and his stern, thick-bearded presence.

Imagine Faith's horror when she heard the music on the downstairs speakers. It was turned up loud, but it wasn't just any music—it was her demo of "It Scares Me." Despite his promise to keep it secret, Chase had played the demo for Morris.

Oh my god! Faith thought.

Then she heard Morris's heavy footsteps bounding up the stairs. "I'm sitting at my desk, and he's walking over toward me, and I remember this so plainly," Faith told Alanna Nash in 1994. "And I'm thinking, *This is it. I'm going to lose my job. Well, I guess it's meant to be. This is probably the kick in the butt I need.* I was just saying all these things in my head, you know, and he walks over and he says, 'You need to get up from behind that desk, and you need to start getting busy. You're not supposed to do this.' And I was like [*Faith sighs*], 'Oh, really!' "

Instead of firing Faith, though, Morris encouraged her to pursue her dream. "You can't believe how hard she worked," Morris's manager Steve Small told *Country Music Weekly* in a 1994 interview. "Not only on her voice by taking singing and acting lessons and studying harmony, but also learning the mechanics of the business, from writing songs to dealing with obsessive fans."

Faith's office encounter with Gary Morris changed her life. It gave her the confidence and encouragement she needed to chase after her dream. Over the next two years, she focused all her energies, outside of her marriage, on learning her craft. She sang on demos for songwriters, she sang backup with various struggling songwriters and would-be artists in the smoky nightclubs of Nashville, and she worked on her appearance, developing her own version of the "big hair" look that was popular with female country artists at the time.

Throughout it all, she pitched the songwriter demos she recorded to producers, record labels, managers, anyone who would take the tape from her extended hand. Those who have never pitched a song or a demo in

Nashville have no idea how brutal it can be. Most of the demo tapes that producers and record executives take from aspiring artists and promise to listen to, end up in the trash can or in a big box that is simply carted away when it fills to the top. In those cases, rejection is offered in the form of silence.

Faith went through dozens, perhaps hundreds of experiences just like that, yet she always picked herself up, smiled, and said, "Thank you." Then she went home and cried a flood of tears and started all over again the next day. Faith wasn't having much success with her music, but she was developing an admirable strength of character that would serve her well in the years to come.

Despite all the good things that were beginning to happen to Faith, she could not shake her obsession with finding her natural mother. She wanted to find her mother every bit as much as she wanted to become a star. Faith's adoptive parents had told her for years that they would not stand in the way—and they were sincere—but they were limited in what they could do. With some pleading, it was Faith's brother Wesley who took on her cause as if it were his own.

Wesley went to the Jackson public library and located a city directory for 1967, the year Faith was born. The book listed the home and employment addresses of every resident of the city, along with each person's Social Security number. Since Ted and Edna knew the natural mother's Social Security number and assorted other details, Wesley searched for the building blocks of his sister's identity. It was tedious, often frustrating work, but he was determined to solve the puzzle.

Going through life as an adopted child is an experience most people will never understand. No matter how much they are loved by their adoptive parents, there is always a place deep inside of them that wants to know every detail of their history. They fantasize about being the children of famous movie stars or recording artists. They fantasize about being the missing heirs of financial empires. And they fantasize about tracking down their natural parents, perhaps wearing a disguise, knocking on their door and pretending to be a salesperson. The possibilities are endless.

Daniel Hill began to see Faith's focus on locating her birth parents as a threat to their marriage. When she came home in tears because some pompous Music Row executive had hurt her feelings, he knew exactly what to say, but when she came home in tears because she wanted to find her birth mother, there were no words that could ease the pain.

After three years of searching, Faith and Wesley were certain they had located Faith's birth mother. They went to the Mississippi judge who had signed the original adoption order and asked her to appoint an intermediary in the event the birth mother did not want to have contact with her daughter. The purpose of an intermediary was to gather a medical history that would be of use to Faith and her children, if she were to have any. If her mother did not want to talk to her, Faith told the judge, then she would interpret it as a sign that a mutual relationship was not meant to be. The judge agreed to name an intermediary.

All that remained now was for the birth mother to be contacted. It was 1990, three years after the search had begun. Faith was no longer a child. She was a twenty-year-old woman. Faith's quest was admittedly selfish. She understood that finding their birth parents was not the answer for all adopted children, but this longing inside of her was so strong that it pushed aside any possibility of empathy for her birth mother.

Faith was too emotional make the call herself, so she asked a friend to do it for her. One can only imagine the torrent of emotions that call generated in Faith's birth mother. Giving a baby up for adoption is never easy. Typically mothers who give their children up for adoption experience feelings of guilt and self-loathing; sometimes those feelings only intensify over the years, regardless of the new families they establish later in life.

To Faith's delight, her birth mother agreed to a meeting with her. "I was a potent mixture of nerves and excitement and anxiety, so many things," Faith told VH1 in an interview. The two of them agreed to meet in a city park that was familiar to both of them. Faith made the eight-hour drive to Jackson and prepared to meet her birth mother.

Faith spotted the woman from a distance and knew immediately that it was her birth mother. The woman was tall, even more statuesque than Faith, and she had blonde hair. She even carried herself with the same awkward grace that came so naturally for Faith. It was like looking in a mirror, only the reflected image was twenty-two years older. At first, Faith could not stop staring at her mother. She had never seen another woman who looked so much like her.

"I found out that she is a painter, an artist, and she has an incredible sense of style," Faith told *Redbook* magazine in 2000. "She's very tall. She's a sweet, sweet woman. I have a lot of respect for her, and I had no feelings of anger or any of that. . . . I know she must have had a lot of love for me to want to give me what she felt was a better choice. Thank God she let me live."

Faith returned to Nashville with a new sense of self. Over the years, she has talked to various publications about her birth parents, but she has told several different versions. She told *Redbook* that her birth mother had eventually married her father. She told Alanna Nash in a 1994 interview that her birth father had been killed in an automobile accident. Add to that Ted and Edna's story that her birth mother had had an affair with a married man. Does it matter which story is correct? Not really. The only reason for mentioning the discrepancies is to point out the obvious: Searches for birth parents almost never end with all the mysteries solved.

For Faith, the meeting with her birth mother offered both pluses and minuses. On the plus side, she obtained access to her medical history and was able to look her mother squarely in the eyes, absorbing whatever degree of spirituality that passed between them. On the minus side, the meeting didn't really change a great deal in her life. She wasn't the daughter of a crown prince or an heiress to a plantation fortune. She was still the same person. She still had the same need for approval and success. She still had Little Elvis inside, pushing her on to bigger and better things.

Unfortunately, Faith's encounter with her birth mother did not automatically provide her with a new extended family. It was probably unrealistic to think that it would. Faith and her birth mother talk occasionally—and Faith always speaks highly of her—but the two women did not develop the close relationship that Faith probably wanted. The reality of adoption is that some doors are sealed shut forever.

⌐ By 1991 Faith was making progress with her career, but it often seemed like the embodiment of that old saying, "Two steps forward, one step back." She hung out at the clubs, particularly the Bluebird Café and Douglas' Corner Café, and she offered her voice to any songwriter who needed a singer for a demo, and she honed her own abilities as a songwriter. She wasn't alone, either. Newcomers, particularly women, seemed to be stepping off the buses in record numbers. Among the new arrivals was a Canadian singer named Shania Twain. She barely caused a ripple when she arrived, but it would be just a matter of time before she rocked Music Row to its knees.

Faith had been in Nashville four years, but her chances of landing a record deal seemed no better today than they did when she arrived. The nightmare of any young singer is that she will wake up one morning and look in the mirror and see the Grand Old Dame of local music, the gutsy broad who dominates the nightclub scene. No female singer ever wants that distinction. Faith was only twenty-four, but she felt ancient. New girls were arriving every day and some of them were getting signed by record labels.

Once she had located her birth mother, Daniel thought her tears would dry up. They didn't. Faith was unhappy in her marriage, but she didn't know what to do about it. She was afraid to stand up for herself and say what she was feeling and thinking. Instead she tried to smooth things over, and denied to herself and to her husband the real cause of her unhappiness.

One of the best things that happened to Faith during this time was striking up a friendship with Gary Burr, a Connecticut-born songwriter who had moved to Nashville in 1989 after making a name for himself as the guitar player for the country-rock band Pure Prairie League. His first big hit was Juice Newton's "Love's Been a Little Bit Hard on Me"; other hits include Garth Brooks's "One Night a Day," Conway Twitty's "That's My Job," and Reba McEntire's "Till You Love Me."

Not many people outside the music industry knew about Burr, but *everyone* on Music Row knew about him. In 1991 alone, he had four Top Ten hits, all recorded by other people: "In a Week" by Diamond Rio;

"Sure Love" by Hal Ketchum; "Watch Me" by Lorrie Morgan; and "Too Busy Being in Love" by Doug Stone.

Burr saw something in Faith others had missed. He encouraged her with her songwriting and he invited her to sing backup with his band in local clubs. One such performance, in 1992 at the Bluebird Café, proved to be fateful. Located in a small, strip-mall shopping center in the Green Hills area of Nashville, the Bluebird is one of the most popular hangouts in the city for songwriters and aspiring artists. It seats just one hundred people, so the fellowship is usually elbow-to-elbow.

In the audience that night was Warner Bros. Records A&R executive Martha Sharp, who had made a name for herself in the mid-1980s with her discovery of Randy Travis. She had worked her way up from secretary to one of the top positions at the record label. Sharp was one of only two female A&R executives in Nashville, but that didn't mean she necessarily opened doors for female performers; on the contrary, she was more likely to sign male recording artists.

That night Sharp went to the Bluebird Café to listen to Gary Burr. She, like most of the music executives in the city, was looking for some excuse to sign him to a recording contract. But that night it was Faith, not Burr, that caught her eye. "She just mesmerized me," Sharp told VH1 in an interview. "I knew she could be a star if she could only halfway sing."

As is usually the case, Faith had no idea she was under scrutiny. Occasionally record executives hear a band or singer and offer them a contract on the spot. However, most of the time they sit back and ponder all the possibilities. Sharp left the Bluebird Café that night feeling pretty good about Faith Hill. Even so, she took her time making up her mind.

Two months later, she ran into Faith at a barbecue. Sharp asked if Faith was working with anyone as far as a solo career was concerned. Faith told her that she and Gary Burr had recorded an eight-track demo to pitch to the record labels. Sharp asked for a copy.

It was the biggest break Faith had received yet, and it could not have possibly come at a better time. On March 22, 1992, Faith had loaded up her 1989 Toyota Camry with all her possessions and moved out of the

Belmont Boulevard home she shared with her husband Daniel. The marriage wasn't working for her. She wanted out.

⌐ After listening to the demo, Martha Sharp wasted no time offering Faith a recording contract with Warner Bros. Records. Sometimes demos are so polished, so nearly complete, that record executives rush albums out as soon as possible. Faith's demo had been recorded in Gary Burr's living room, so technically it was not meant to be anything other than a raw vehicle for the songs.

Sharp decided to take her time with Faith. Female singers were still a tough sell with radio and the good-ole-boy network on Music Row, especially if they were very attractive. Sharp's first impression of Faith—namely, that she was so beautiful that she could become a star "if she could only halfway sing"—dictated both the style of music Sharp chose for the singer and the pace at which she would be developed. Faith was already a star in Sharp's eyes. It became her task to find the music that would match that level of star-brightness.

Sharp's first priority was to find a producer to work with Faith, someone who could develop her existing talents and encourage her to move in new directions, particularly toward more pop-oriented crossover material. She approached Scott Hendricks, who had produced hit albums for Alan Jackson, and Brooks and Dunn. In Sharp's eyes, Hendricks possessed two essential ingredients: the ability to produce a commercial album, and the ability to communicate with Faith in the studio without appearing overbearing.

Hendricks had no track record working with female artists, but Sharp counted on his easygoing, self-effacing manner to make Faith comfortable in the studio. Everyone who met Faith during those years spoke about her in similar terms: There was something fragile about her, something that could break if not handled properly. Gary Burr once described her as someone he wanted to protect. Sharp wanted to protect her, too.

Hendricks agreed to work with Faith, and, after a meeting with him, Faith gave a thumbs-up. First they would have to locate songs—Faith already had ideas about that; her friend Gary Burr was one of the best tunesmiths in the city—then they would have to work on her style, the way she phrased key words in a song and interpreted the material. There was also the matter of the Little Elvis that lived inside Faith. Sharp didn't know its name, but she knew that whatever it was, it was the exact opposite of the fragile, birdlike perception of Faith that she wanted to protect. Hendricks would have to be gentle enough to inspire Faith and tough enough to keep Little Elvis in line.

During this gut-wrenching creative process, Faith felt like an emotional train wreck. She had invested five years in her marriage and breaking up was hard to do. Her entire life she had been a facilitator, the person who nurtured those around her. The very thought of hurting someone's feelings was enough to bring her to tears.

Sharp's next challenge was to find a manager for Faith. Usually by the time performers are signed to recording contracts, they have acquired a manager to protect their interests. That wasn't the case with Faith. She had representation in the sense that she took her contract from Warner Bros. Records to a lawyer before signing it, but she had no one to look after the day-to-day business of her career. The most logical choice for her would have been Reba McEntire's husband, Narvel Blackstock, who headed up Starstruck Entertainment, but Faith was reluctant to go there, primarily because she felt he already had his hands full managing the careers of Reba and her protégée, Linda Davis.

Although Faith felt pressured to sign with a manager—Warner Bros. Records certainly didn't want her managing her own career, not considering the money they expected to invest in her—she delayed making a decision until she was certain there would actually be a CD headed for the stores. Besides, making a commitment to a manager was not unlike making a commitment to a husband. Something inside Faith told her to go slow.

As work progressed in the studio, Warner Bros. Records' publicity department began looking for opportunities to put the spotlight on its rising star. When they learned that Gary Morris would be the guest host for TNN's popular program *Nashville Now* in November 1992, they asked him if he would be interested in having Faith on the show.

It was Faith's first television performance. Wearing a brightly colored floral-print dress, Faith sang a song with the show's band, slightly rushing through it, then joined Morris at the interview desk. Morris beamed with obvious pride and told viewers that she was about to become a household name. Faith nervously flashed a smile at the studio audience and confessed that it was her very first television show. Asked by Morris what she thought about being on television, she replied, "I like it!"

Impressed by Faith's performance, the Nashville office of Warner Bros. Records sent a tape of the show to executives at the West Coast office. Within the record label, there was quite a buzz about the dazzling strawberry-blonde from Star, Mississippi. Warner Bros. realized that how they packaged Faith would be crucial to the success of her albums. The only thing that bothered them was her reluctance to sign with a manager.

Carl Scott, one of the Warner Bros. Records executives on the West Coast, gave the TNN tape to Gary Borman, a Los Angeles manager who represented another of the label's country-music stars, Dwight Yoakam. Scott told Borman he felt it would be a good match. Borman said he was interested and would fly to Nashville to check her out.

That Christmas, Faith went home to be with her parents. To her surprise, Borman called her while she was in Star. "We talked, and I loved him over the phone," Faith told Alanna Nash. "He was a family man, and he was really, really smart, and I thought, man, it was just exciting. I had not gotten that excited about any manager I'd talked to—and I'm learning to go more with my gut."

Faith told Borman that she would be performing at a Warner Bros. showcase at the Ace of Clubs, a downtown Nashville nightspot. When he saw her in the club that evening, he was knocked out by her big voice and her pretty, innocent face.

Borman introduced himself to Faith there in the club. He made a favorable first impression on her, but she was reluctant to make a commitment—and with good reason. Borman had only two country acts, Dwight Yoakam and Mary Chapin Carpenter. The remainder of his clients were rock 'n' roll acts.

Faith had lived in Nashville long enough to know that it was risky going to management outside the city. She was a Southern girl who sang Southern music. Could she trust her art to a man who didn't live in the South and didn't have a reputation for working with Southern artists?

Dwight Yoakam was a big star but he was not held in high regard in Nashville (at least not musically), where he was considered more of a novelty act than a serious country artist. Mary Chapin Carpenter, on the other hand, was well regarded on Music Row, but the New Jersey–born graduate of Brown University was never considered a member of the Nashville inner circle.

Gary Borman presented a dilemma to Faith: If she planned to remain a country singer, he would be the worst possible choice, for the simple reason that he was an outsider, someone who would alienate Music Row power brokers. If, on the other hand, she planned to become a crossover artist, someone who had hits on the pop charts, and perhaps later wanted to move into movies and television, then he would be perfect.

Faith told Borman she would have to think about it a while longer.

Take Me as I Am

On March 2, 1993, Faith made her official debut at the Warner Bros. Records Nashville Superstars show at the Grand Ole Opry auditorium. The event was part of the industry-wide program put together for the Country Radio Seminar. It was traditional for each of the major record labels to showcase their talent for the program directors, announcers, and sales executives who gathered each year in Nashville to talk shop and receive preview performances from up-and-coming stars.

Twenty-five-year-old Faith Hill was a nervous wreck, even more so than when she had taken the stage a decade earlier for the Raleigh, Mississippi, tobacco spit. Although the Superstars show was not an Opry function, the auditorium is magical in the way it can suck the air out of a singer's lungs by virtue of its glorious past. That mystique would be stressful enough on a new singer, but add to that an audience composed of the radio executives who can make or break that singer's career and it is easy to understand why no recording artist in her right mind would consider her performance there as just another gig.

There was added pressure because the March 1993 issue of *Country America* magazine was already on the stands with a cover story titled "Meet the 12 Best New Singers of '93." Included were brief biographies and photos of Joy White, Lari White, Shania Twain, Lisa Stewart, John Michael Montgomery, DeAnna Cox, Tracy Byrd, Tim Mensy, Robert Ellis Orrall, Stacy Dean Campbell, Radney Foster, and Tim McGraw.

"Who'll be country's next Garth, or its new Reba, its hottest new stars of 1993?" asked the magazine. "We took a close look at the current crowd of newcomers and put our bets down on these dozen young performers. They've definitely got the goods—the talent, the polish and the all-important industry backing—to make it big. Now all they need are the breaks."

Every new country artist in Nashville was spotlighted by the magazine, it seemed, *except* Faith Hill. It was just the sort of thing that causes trouble in the inner sanctum of a record label, as doubts and recriminations among insecure executives are raised about an artist's commercial appeal.

Faith sang two songs that evening—"Take Me as I Am" and "Wild One"—and when she walked off the stage she was numb all over. "I swear, I can't tell you anything about it," she later told Craig Peters of *CountryBeat* magazine. "Except I saw the 'WSM Grand Ole Opry,' you know, on the microphone there. That's all I can remember. I was so nervous!"

A few weeks after her showcase performance, Faith signed a management contract with Gary Borman. It would be the first of two life-altering decisions she would make that year.

Still separated from her husband Daniel, Faith focused all her efforts on her upcoming album. Working with producer Scott Hendricks was better than she ever imagined it could be. He never pushed her too hard, screamed at her, or berated her in the studio when she made mistakes. He had a very ponderous, almost professorial way about him that counterbalanced Faith's more emotional approach to music.

Part of their studio chemistry was due to the fact that both had similar backgrounds. Hendricks was a small-town boy from Clinton, Oklahoma (population 9,298), who was not unlike the "awe, shucks" screen image of actor James Stewart; he had a sense of right and wrong that was imbued with the old-fashioned family values of rural Oklahoma. Faith knew a country boy when she saw one, and she saw that quality right away in Hendricks.

He went out of his way to accommodate her. When she complained that the studio was too cold, he turned up the heat so that she could be comfortable, even though that went against what later became myth in a digital age: namely, that studios had to be kept cold so the raised temperature would not "mess up" the analog tape.

Working in a studio is just the opposite of working a live performance. Everything is done in bits and pieces in the studio (another reason why someone of Hendricks's temperament is important). Before you ever even go into the studio, you have to listen to dozens of demo tapes, especially if the artist is not herself a songwriter, to find just the right song mix for the album. Then you have to decide on the instrumentation that will be needed to make the music come alive.

Once that preparatory work is complete, the producer can begin laying down the musical tracks for each song. That usually involves just the rhythm section (drums, guitar, bass, and piano). If the singer wants to be present, she will sing what are called "scratch vocals." They are done simply to give guidance to the band and to allow the singer to experiment with intonation and accent. Later, they are "scratched" from the tape to make room for the final vocals. Once all that has been done, specialized musicians such as horn players, slide guitarists, and backup singers are brought in to provide yet another layer to the music.

While the early stage of this process was going on, Faith worked with a number of Nashville songwriters to compile material for the album. She looked at songwriting as if it were a full-time job. She did it every day, reflecting the Mississippi blue-collar work ethic that if something is worth doing, it is worth doing well. Writing was a new experience for her, but like everything else she did, she threw herself into it with a passion. Before the year ended, she would write more than twenty songs.

Creatively she was growing like an out-of-control weed. She became what television talk-show host Oprah Winfrey likes to call an "empowered woman." It was during this time she found that she was attracted to Hendricks. At six feet two inches, he towered over her in a way that diminished her own height and made her feel secure. Not only did they share the same small-town values, they shared a confidence in Faith's dream of stardom. Within a matter of weeks they had formed an intimate friendship that would soon blossom into a full-blown romance.

By summer, Faith had made a decision about her marriage to Daniel. On July 28, 1993, she hired a lawyer in a high-powered Nashville law firm and filed for divorce, citing "irreconcilable differences." It was a tough thing for her to do, considering the nurturing role she had played in the relationship, but she felt she had no other choice. It was time to end one life and begin another.

Also at the 1993 Country Radio Seminar with Faith Hill at the Grand Ole Opry earlier in the year, was new Mercury Records artist Shania Twain. Of all the new female artists waiting in the wings, it was Shania who eventually would have the biggest impact on Faith's career, though no one could have imagined that at the time.

Like Faith, Shania was branded an outsider when she arrived in Nashville. Shania's hometown of Timmins, Ontario, Canada, was every bit as foreign to Music Row as was Star, Mississippi. Actually, despite the population difference—Timmins has a population of over forty thousand—the two communities have more in common with each other than they do with Nashville.

Timmins, Ontario, is a blue-collar city in which most of the jobs center around its gold and zinc mines and its proximity to the Canadian bush. Located four hundred miles north of Toronto, it is viewed by many as a jumping-off place for the arctic wilderness. As a teen Shania worked in the bush with her stepfather; usually she was the only female in the crew. Even though the work was hard—and the men outnumbered her twelve to one—she thrived in that environment. In a 1993 interview with this author, she said that what she missed most about Canada was the wilderness. "I used to spend a lot of time canoeing," she said. "I grew up doing those things so, to me, not having access to the freshwater lakes and just walking through the bush is [something I miss]."

Beside her rural upbringing, Shania had something else in common

Faith and video
director Steven
Goldman accept
a CMA award
for "This Kiss."

Faith performs
at the 1998
Country Music
Association Awards.

Faith and Amy Grant are teammates at a charity event.

Faith and teammate Barbara Mandrell go up against Lisa Stewart at a 1993 charity event.

Faith with Warner Bros.
executive Martha Sharp.
© ALAN L. MAYOR

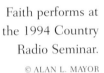

Faith performs at
the 1994 Country
Radio Seminar.
© ALAN L. MAYOR

Faith on stage at the
1994 Georgia Music
Festival.   © ALAN L. MAYOR

Faith performs with Vince Gill at a fund-raiser
for Belmont University in Nashville (1993).

Faith and producer
Scott Hendricks
celebrate the success
of "Wild One."

Faith and Tim kiss after performing "Let's Make Love" at the 2000 Academy of Country Music Awards.

REUTERS/FRED POUSER/ARCHIVE PHOTOS

Faith reacts to the audience at Pixelon.com's iBASH '99.

REUTERS/ETHAN MILLER/ARCHIVE PHOTOS

Faith and Tim win the "Vocal Event of the Year" award from the Country Music Association for the song "It's Your Love."

© ALAN L. MAYOR

Faith arrives at the taping of the VH1 special "VH1 Divas 2000." REUTERS/BRAD RICKERBY/ARCHIVE PHOTOS

Faith takes the stage
at the VH1 tribute
to Diana Ross.
REUTERS/JEFF CHRISTENSEN/
ARCHIVE PHOTOS

Faith, Diana Ross, and Mariah Carey harmonize at the VH1 special.
REUTERS/JEFF CHRISTENSEN/ARCHIVE PHOTOS

Faith gathers a crowd of 10,000 at the Jackson, Mississippi Zoo performance (2000).

JAMES L. DICKERSON

Faith gives Brother Dyess a thumbs up while singing "This Kiss."

JAMES L. DICKERSON

with Faith. In 1987, the year Faith moved to Nashville, Shania's parents were killed when their Chevy Suburban rammed head-on into a logging truck. Shania was traumatized by the event. Not only did she lose her mother and stepfather, she found herself the surrogate parent of her three teenage siblings. She supported them by working as a cabaret singer in the resort communities in northern Ontario. How ironic that Shania and Faith—both driven women in search of a lost maternal identity—would become the two biggest country-music stars in history. Perhaps they needed us as much as we needed them.

By the time Shania arrived in Nashville, she had been bruised emotionally by life's cruel surprises. It required a great deal of focus and resolve to put that aside so she could do what she needed to do with her career. She handled the cultural differences she encountered in Nashville with grace and good humor, but adapting to the music culture proved somewhat more difficult.

From the beginning, Mercury Records had problems getting radio to air Shania's music. Program directors just weren't interested. As a result her first release, "What Made You Say That," never rose above number 55 on the singles charts. Two other new artists on the label, John Brannen and Toby Keith, were experiencing similar problems.

Instead of sending those new acts out on the road to open for established stars, the record label decided to group them together and market them as the "Triple Play Tour." The tour wasn't a huge success, but it did attract attention to the artists and gave Shania her first opportunity to perform before American audiences.

Shania knew during the tour that her first single wasn't doing well, so when her Canadian manager Mary Bailey called and told her that movie actor Sean Penn had agreed to direct the video for her next single, "Dance with the One that Brought You," she was encouraged. They spent a couple of weeks talking about the video, but when the time came to shoot it in Los Angeles, they found they only needed one day to wrap it up. No one was surprised more than Shania with the way the session went.

By the end of the summer it was clear that "Dance with the One that Brought You" would not make it into the Top 50, despite the video's association with Sean Penn. A third single, "You Lay a Whole Lot of Love on Me," was released in the fall, but it never made it onto the charts.

By the end of 1993, Shania's future as a recording artist seemed to be in doubt, to everyone except Shania and her record label. Mercury Records stuck with Shania because they believed in her as a recording artist and because they believed the music industry was not addressing the needs of female CD-buyers. Working together, Shania and Mercury Records would bring about a revolution in country music that ultimately would affect every female singer and record label in the city—especially Faith Hill.

One can only imagine the songs that Faith and producer Scott Hendricks turned down for her debut album. The songs that made the final cut seemed remarkably autobiographical and fit together like complementary colors in an abstract painting. Taken as a whole, they clearly reflected the powerful emotions she had experienced over the past five years. They made a strong statement—to Faith herself if to no one else.

"Wild One," co-written by Jaime Kyle, Pat Bunch, and Will Rambeaux, is an up-tempo song about a wild child with an angel's face who has dreams and the courage to seek them out. "Take Me as I Am," written by Bob Dipiero and Karen Staley, is a harmony-driven tune about a woman who hopes that a man with a gentle hand will take her as she is and not try to make her into someone else.

"I Would Be Stronger than That," written by Faith's friend Gary Burr, tells the story of a woman who reaches out for help with a troubled relationship. She proclaims that she loves her partner; that now wouldn't be a good time to leave; and that she is sure one day he'll change. Faith sings that she hopes she would be stronger than that. The song had been previously recorded by Irish-born singer Maura O'Connell, who became an outsider in Nashville because of her passion to push the musical envelope, but none of that mattered to Faith, who took the song and made it her own.

Faith first heard "I Would Be Stronger than That" at the Bluebird

Café during one of Burr's performances. "The first time I heard that song, I could just feel someone being in that situation where they could not get out of," she told Alanna Nash, then corrected herself for fear the writer would think she herself had had similar problems. "That's not happened to me, but I could just feel someone being in a situation that they could not get out of. That's probably the worst feeling in the world. So when I heard [Gary Burr] doing it in the round with this acoustic guitar . . . he played that, and I just, tears were just rolling down my face. It just really moved me, and I said, *I hope and pray that some day I get to record that song.*"

When Faith suggested the song to Hendricks, he was cool to the idea. He suggested they discuss it with Martha Sharp in her office. At first the producer and the record executive were opposed to including the song. They suggested that Faith hold on to it for her second album.

"Just let me try," Faith pleaded.

They hated to say no, but business was business.

With that, Faith started singing. Sitting in a chair across the desk from Sharp, she poured her heart into the song, her eyes lost in the poetry of the music. To Sharp's surprise, she sang the song all the way through. Faith can be very persuasive when she wants to be.

Producer and executive looked at each other, their logic suddenly made insignificant.

"Okay, we'll do it," they said.

Burr wrote and co-wrote two additional songs on the album, "Just About Now" and "Just Around the Eyes," which he co-produced with Michael Clute. "Just About Now," a middle-of-the-road ballad about surviving the present, could have been written with Faith in mind.

By the time work began in the studio, Faith had co-written twenty songs, but only two of them made it onto the album, "I've Got This Friend" and "Go the Distance." The latter song she co-wrote with Trey Bruce, a talented songwriter from Memphis who is the son of actor Ed Bruce (the star of *The Last Days of Frank and Jessie James* and *Fire Down Below*). "I've Got This Friend," which Faith co-wrote with Bruce Burch and Vern Dant, was recorded as a duet with Larry Stewart. He also did background vocals on the album, along with Lari White, who was one of the twelve newcomers *Country America* magazine had picked for stardom in March 1993.

The most interesting song to come out of Faith's first sessions was "Piece of My Heart," originally recorded in the summer of 1968 by Big Brother and the Holding Company. With blues-rock legend Janis Joplin providing the lead vocals, the song was one of the big hits of that year (Faith was only one year old). Joplin's biggest hit was "Me and Bobby McGee," but "Piece of My Heart" remained her most popular concert song.

Incredibly, Faith had never even heard Joplin's version. She chose the song after hearing a country version that James House had recorded in Nashville for a demo. When she finally heard Joplin's version she was speechless.

"I was like, *I can't believe that we have taken that song and made a country record from it*," she confided to Alanna Nash. "I'm very thankful I didn't listen to it before because I really would have been influenced by it. When people asked me, 'What are you recording on your record?' and I'd say Janis Joplin's 'Piece of My Heart' . . . their faces would fall, and they'd say, 'You're *really* doing "Piece of My Heart"? That was her anthem song.' And I'd think, *Oh no! Maybe I shouldn't have done it!*"

By the fall of 1993, Faith's first album had been recorded. With the music in the can, now came the hard part—creating an image to accompany the music. The first task was to compose a cover for the CD. In keeping with Martha Sharp's initial impression of Faith as an artist whose good looks would be a major part of record sales, the photographer created a series of "glamour" images. Faith was clothed in a tight green dress and her face was caked with makeup. They put her hair in a style she had never worn and she was asked to become someone she didn't recognize.

When Faith saw the photographs, she hated them. She told manager Gary Borman that she didn't feel comfortable with that type of image. It just wasn't who she was. Borman agreed with her and convinced Warner Bros. to schedule a second session.

So they sent her back into the studio instructing the photographer to do "whatever she wants to do." Faith wore faded jeans and a white shirt to the session, and when the photographer saw her, he declared her casual outfit perfect for the shoot. The only thing the photographer suggested was that she take off her shoes. That was the kind of compromise that Faith understood. The end result was a cover photo that depicted Faith for what she was—a small-town girl with bright, dreamy eyes and a broad, picture-perfect smile.

After consulting with Faith and her manager Gary Borman, Warner Bros. executive Martha Sharp decided that the first single would be "Wild One." At first, it was a toss-up between "Wild One" and "Take Me as I Am," but the latter seemed a little too safe for a first release and they decided to go with a song that had an edgier sound.

It is customary for record labels to send radio stations a sampler that contains a limited number of songs. They do that several months before the album is released so that their promotions departments can "work" a single song without the distractions offered by an entire album. That logic is usually sound. It is most difficult to achieve a hit record if radio stations all across the country are airing different songs from the album. It has the effect, so to speak, of splitting the vote.

Warner Bros. chose four songs for Faith's sampler, including "Wild One" and "Piece of My Heart." As they were shipped to radio stations coast-to-coast, Faith headed back to Star, Mississippi. Accompanying her was a television production crew from Nashville. The Warner Bros. publicity machine had arranged an "event" that could be exploited for its promotional value: Faith would sing the National Anthem at a Tigers football game. It was a natural. Faith, the former cheerleader, the hometown girl made good, going home to celebrate her success.

Actually, it was more than just a football game. It was the homecoming game, the biggest event of the year, outside of Thanksgiving and Christmas, for both the school and the community. Everyone made a big deal out of Faith singing the National Anthem. They gathered around her and congratulated her on her success (she already had sent home cassette copies of "Wild One" to selected friends).

McLaurin Attendance Center student Jennifer Byrd—a Faith Hill look-alike with a bubbly personality—was only nine years old at the time, but the event made such an impression on her that she remembers it clearly. "She had blonde, curly hair, and she was really skinny," recalled Byrd, who is now sixteen. "She's made it big-time and I like the way she's handled her life." More recently Faith sent the school one of her dresses to be auctioned off for a fundraiser. "I tried the dress on to see how it would feel," Byrd beamed.

During the homecoming-game visit, Faith met with baseball coach Charlie Butts. To his surprise, she thanked him for encouraging her to follow her dreams. "When she said that, I couldn't remember doing that," said Butts. "In twenty-six years, I have taught thousands and thousands of students. When she told me that, it made me realize how much influence [a teacher] can have on students and not even realize it. She told me that she had told me about [her decision] to go to Nashville, and I said, 'You need to follow your dreams. Don't hesitate.'"

Coach Butts's dreams are measured in terms of winning seasons, athletic scholarships, and recruiters from the majors. He has never thought of himself as a coach who sent players on the field of life to chase after their dreams. Yet that's exactly what he did with Faith Hill. He said the right words at the right time, and Faith clung to those words when most of those around her ridiculed her and tried to talk her out of her dreams.

"I guess it showed some maturity on her part to even seek out advice," Butts says. "I am honored that she came to me. I'm pretty strict with my players and classrooms. Maybe she saw that I was always trying to teach the kids about life. I'm not so concerned about what they learn about Egypt or the pyramids as I am what kind of citizens they will be when they get out of school."

What Faith has accomplished is so far against the odds of probability that it seems mathematically impossible. "It was a little bit unrealistic," he admits. "But she was naive enough to believe that she could make it. As a teacher, I'm not going to say, 'Faith, that's too hard.'" Coach Butts grinned. "I do reflect back now and say to myself, *You'd better be careful what you say to these kids.*"

⌒ That winter Faith flew to Los Angeles, California, to film her first video. The site of the video shoot was near Simi Valley, about an hour's drive northwest of Los Angeles. Traveling in a mini-caravan, Faith set out from the city with the director, crew members, and representatives of her record label. With most of Faith's entourage in the lead van, she was surrounded by strangers in the second van. There wasn't much conversation, so Faith sat quietly and looked out the window at the passing countryside. Silence can be contagious, especially where celebrities are concerned. No one wants to outtalk the star.

Suddenly Faith saw something familiar. Off the road was a house that looked as comforting as her parents' home in Star. "That looks just like Laura Ingalls' house!" she said, breaking the silence with her excited voice.

"That *is* Laura Ingalls' house," answered one of the men in the van, explaining that it was where the popular television show was filmed.

"Oh my gosh! Oh my gosh!" Faith exclaimed, bouncing on the seat like a small child. "We've got to go back and get a picture!"

Dutifully the van driver stopped, turned around, and drove back to where Faith had first spotted the house. They all got out of the van to gaze at the famous television house, but they didn't approach it. Faith took a photograph or two, then they got back into the van and continued their journey to the video site.

"I didn't go up and walk around, but I wanted to," Faith told Alanna Nash several weeks after the incident. "We were tight for time, but I'm telling you, that was the coolest thing! It was so small . . . I loved that show. I still cry every time I see those shows. I'd like to get a collection of them, if they ever make them."

Told by Nash that videocassettes of the shows were being marketed on television, Faith said, "Are you serious? I've gotta get those—they don't have shows like that anymore—those shows will teach you values and morals and stuff."

When Faith returned to Nashville, she discovered that the Warner Bros. "glamour squad" had struck again, this time with an idea for a calendar that put more of a focus on her photogenic face than on her music. Faith was opposed to the idea, but she went along with it, perhaps because she didn't want to appear to be difficult to work with.

When the calendar was released, it attracted nearly as much attention as her album. That was exactly what Faith had feared would happen. More than once she was forced to convince interviewers that she was not just some model who recorded an album.

"The calendar was someone's idea at Warner Bros., and I don't think any pictures in there are offensive to women," she explained to Nash. "So I think it was just someone's idea that, 'Yeah, we'll try that. The album's already out.' . . . I get embarrassed and upset when somebody says—and this is hard for me to say this—'Oh, you're really pretty!' That's not the first thing I want to hear. [My album] is what I've wanted to do all my life, and I've worked really hard."

Faith returned to Star to be with her family at Christmas. So much had changed since she first moved to Nashville. She had left with stars in her eyes and no emotional entanglements. She had brimmed with optimism over her potential for success and the possible fruits of her quest for her natural mother. The future was a prize to be won with hard work, smart decisions, and lots of prayers.

Seven years later, she still had stars in her eyes, but much of her life had changed radically. She had to tell her family for the first time that she had filed for divorce. They knew about the separation, of course, but, like most parents, they had hoped Faith and Daniel would be able to work it out. Faith didn't tell them that she was falling in love again—but why would she?

Then there was the matter of locating her birth mother. While that story had a happy ending in that she had been able to meet with the woman who had given birth to her, it had not resulted in a magical understanding of her place in the world. For years she had thought that her life would be transformed by that moment. That hadn't happened, and it had left her with an entire new set of mysteries about herself.

It was during this visit that she began to see her family in a new light. They seemed more noble *and* more flawed—not that the latter was a negative quality in Faith's eyes. Their flaws made them even more noble in her eyes. For example, after Christmas dinner that year, Edna rose from the table to get that paragon of Southern deserts—thick, gooey, delicious Karo pecan pie.

"My mom puts whipped cream on it, and [my dad] goes over and he says, 'There's no more whupped cream!' " Faith recalled to Alanna Nash. "He says 'whupped.' I've been around people who have corrected me before, in my relationship, where I was corrected about what I said, and I thought, *I don't like that.* That may be a silly example, but to me, that's just precious—and there's so little of that around anymore. So I'm very fortunate to be from a small town."

For the first time in her life, Faith looked at who she was and she was proud. Ever since arriving in Nashville she had been made to feel inferior because of her humble background. Her husband had not been the only person to correct her when she said things that were wrong, by Nashville standards, and she had carried that burden for the longest time. Now everything was beginning to look different.

What was wrong with asking the world to look at itself through her eyes? Faith knew things that others didn't know. She knew about the Little Elvis inside of her and she knew that when he finally got his way, there would be hell to pay by the doubters. With all that in mind, she looked at the world—and at her loving family gathered around the Christmas table—and she uttered the words that could well have been used as the battle cry for her upcoming media campaign: "Pass the whupped cream, please."

⟶ When Faith returned to Nashville after Christmas, she got a major surprise: "Wild One" was moving up the charts at the speed of light. Early on, they had had a problem with the sampler because many radio stations pulled "Piece of My Heart" off the disk and played it as the single instead of "Wild One." The record label reversed that trend by promising to release "Piece of My Heart" as a single at a later date.

By the first week in January 1994, Faith had a number-one record on the charts. "Wild One" held the top spot for four consecutive weeks, making her the first female country star to have a single do so since 1964. A number-one record is a major achievement. Keeping it at number-one for four weeks is considered akin to walking on water.

While this was great news for Warner Bros., it created a dilemma for the record label insofar as the release of the second single was concerned. If they picked the wrong song, it would be disastrous for the album. They decided to play it safe.

Since they already knew that "Piece of My Heart" was popular with radio, they tapped it for the second release. Although critics were brutal in their comments about the song, usually commenting on Faith's brashness in doing a country remake of a rock classic, it quickly went to number one on the charts.

Faith was horrified that critics would say such negative things about the song—didn't they understand that she was a nice person who was just following her dream?—but she was pleased that radio had a different opinion. The fact that different people could have polar-opposite reactions to her songs mystified her. She still had a lot to learn about the music business.

The same month that "Piece of My Heart" peaked at number one, a new music magazine titled *Country Weekly* hit the newsstands. Its premier issue had a photograph of Garth Brooks on the cover—but it also featured a new artist, Faith Hill, with the headline "From Secretary to Superstar." It was the first time Faith had heard the S-word applied to her career. Inside, the magazine did an impressive two-page story about her. She told the magazine that music had become for her a way of "healing hurts."

That was a phrase that was on Faith's mind quite a bit during this time. On February 23, 1994, her divorce from Daniel Hill was finalized in the Fourth Circuit Court of Davidson County. Under the terms of the divorce, Faith was allowed to keep her 1989 Toyota Camry (obviously not all superstars ride around in limousines) and Daniel was given their Toyota 4-Runner. In addition, Daniel kept their house on Belmont Boulevard.

The proceedings had not gone as smoothly as Faith had hoped. You would think that after seven years of marriage Faith would be able to walk away with more than a 1989 Toyota Camry and the clothes on her back. In fact, Daniel demanded that she pay him a form of alimony, although it was not described as such in the court documents.

Faith agreed to pay Daniel a record royalty participation in her debut album that was calculated as follows: Daniel would be paid $25,000 when *Take Me as I Am* reached sales of half a million units, and an additional $25,000 for each half-million units sold thereafter.

That wasn't all, either. Daniel demanded—and received—a 50-percent share of all the royalties earned from the twenty songs she had co-written while they were married. Included were two of the songs on her album, "I've Got This Friend" and "Go the Distance." Others were "This Foolish Heart," which she co-wrote with Gary Burr and Kathy Majesty; "Far Away from Here," co-written with Pamela Hayes; "Hold On for Dear Life," co-written with Barry Alfonzo; "Tears of Sara Jane," co-written with Liz Hengber and Shana Harrington; "Heart Mender," co-written with Anthony Smith and Michael Garvin; and "I Can't Wait Forever," co-written with Eric Silver.

The fact that Faith would agree to such an arrangement shows how desperate she was to get out of the marriage. She has never commented publicly about the terms of the divorce, and attempts to reach Daniel have been unsuccessful (he has since left his job at PolyGram). Presumably Daniel made these demands because he had supported her while she worked on the songs. Faith walked out of that seven-year marriage with no compensation for the love, companionship, and affection she had offered him, other than a six-year-old vehicle, but at least she had her freedom and, judging from the titles of the songs she wrote while married to him, that was a gift of monumental proportions.

⟿ The first week in October is one of the most important of the year to country recording artists. That is when the Country Music Association presents its entertainment awards during a weeklong celebration that attracts worldwide interest.

Nominated for the 1994 "Horizon Award" was Faith Hill, along with newcomers Martina McBride, John Michael Montgomery, Lee Roy Parnell, and Tim McGraw. The award is given to the new artist the association feels is most deserving of recognition.

An eighteen-page special supplement of the Nashville *Tennessean*, labeled "Hot Ticket," was devoted to the upcoming CMA awards show. It featured Faith on the front cover, along with John Michael Montgomery and Wynonna Judd.

In a telephone interview Faith told the newspaper that one of the highlights of the year for her had been opening for Reba McEntire. The first show they did together was special, she said. "I remember going out in the audience and just sitting out there watching Reba doing her dress rehearsal. And I was sitting there thinking, *I'm about to open for this woman*. And I just burst into tears."

Faith performed during the CMA awards show, but she did not win the Horizon Award. That honor went to John Michael Montgomery, whose two million–selling *Kickin' It Up* album was the talk of the town. The odds were stacked against Faith from the beginning. In the fourteen years the Horizon Award had been presented, it had gone to female singers on only three occasions. Also a loser that year was Reba McEntire, who had been nominated in two categories—Entertainer of the Year and Female Vocalist of the Year. Those awards were taken home by Vince Gill and Pam Tillis, respectively.

After the show, Faith did what all country stars do when they are rebounding from an unpleasant personal experience (in this case a divorce): she hit the road. Before the year was over, she would perform in over one hundred cities, beginning with a sold-out appearance with Alan Jackson later that very week at Middle Tennessee State University.

It was an exhausting schedule, but at the same time it was liberating, for it put her in touch with the fans she had dreamed about for most of her life. The little girl singing behind closed doors with a hairbrush was now onstage in full view of people who loved and appreciated her.

One day, as they drove through Wisconsin on their way to an interview at a radio station, they decided to stop at a convenience store to get something to eat. Faith was standing at the candy counter, looking over the merchandise, when she became aware of someone watching her. She looked up and saw that the store clerk was staring at her.

Faith was horrified. Her heart started pounding. Her first thought, as she later explained it, was that the clerk thought she was trying to steal a candy bar. The haunting guilt of the candy bar she had stolen in her youth was overpowering. Quickly she picked up a candy bar and took it to the counter where the hawk-eyed clerk stood watching her every move. Faith dropped the candy bar to the counter, wondering if she should deny that she was trying to steal it or if she should simply act as if nothing was wrong.

The clerk broke out into a broad smile, and said, "You're the Wild One, aren't you?"

Faith froze, not sure how to answer that question. Finally, an unsure Faith stuck out her hand: "My name is Faith Hill."

At that point, both women screamed with delight.

"It's like for fifteen minutes or so we were both going, 'Oh, gosh, I can't believe this!' " Faith later recalled. "Just giggling, you know. It was really funny."

In the weeks that followed, Faith would be inundated with fan letters. Some were from prisoners who had seen her video in prison. Others were from people who had been moved by her music. One letter was from a woman who said she had never written a fan letter and wasn't sure that her letter would qualify as a fan letter, but she wanted to tell Faith what had happened when she had listened to Faith's album for the first time.

The woman explained that she had been driving in her car, and when the last song on the album, "I Would Be Stronger than That," came on, she started crying so hard that she had to pull off the road and stop. She went on to explain that she had a friend who was going through the same thing as the woman in the song and when she heard the pain and confusion expressed so beautifully in the song it was more than she could bear.

When Faith read the letter, she broke down and cried.

⌒

Once Faith's divorce was finalized, the relationship that had been whispered about for months blossomed into full public view. Faith and producer Scott Hendricks became Nashville's newest power couple.

Intimate relationships between female singers and male producers have existed for as long as there have been recording machines, but usually they are short in duration and seldom progress beyond the gossip stage among studio technicians. That's because female artists historically have saved their hearts for other recording artists or successful businessmen who have high profiles within the industry. Stardom is addictive. Once an artist has experienced its power, they are more likely to be attracted to individuals who have star power of their own.

Scott Hendricks was not a star, but within the cohesive Nashville music industry he was considered a starmaker, and that was enough to turn heads. "Anyone who saw the couple together realized that Scott loved Faith with schoolboy devotion, relishing her every word and gesture, seeing in her the embodiment of everything he ever wanted in a woman," wrote author Laurence Leamer. "He had left his wife and marriage to start anew, and his new life was with Faith."

Beyond Nashville's inner circle, Faith's love life became the topic of gossip and speculation. Inquiring reporters, especially those she encountered out on the road, almost always asked if she was dating anyone. Her answer was always yes, she was dating "someone special." Depending on her mood, she might also say that she hoped that her "someone special" would someday put a ring on her finger.

Sometimes the gossip took a different twist. Toward the end of 1994, Faith sang the National Anthem at a Dallas Cowboys game, after which rumors circulated that Faith was dating Cowboys quarterback Troy Aikman. Both Faith and Aikman denied the romance, but gossip columnists knew a good story when they heard one and they continued to write stories about the alleged romance.

Scott was troubled by the rumors, but he was in love with Faith and trusted her. One day, while he was working in the studio, he received a telephone call from Aikman. The quarterback told the producer he felt badly about the rumors and wanted to assure him there was no romance between the two of them. As a goodwill gesture, Aikman offered Scott two tickets to the upcoming Super Bowl in Miami, which pitted San Francisco against San Diego. Scott accepted the tickets. Why Aikman would feel obliged to intervene in a relationship between two people he did not know has never been explained, but the fact that he did created a climate in which a genuine friendship developed between the singer and the athlete.

By December, gossip was the least of Faith's problems. Her touring schedule, a constant stream of one-nighters, was grueling. Added to that were the many interviews she was doing on the road. When she wasn't singing, it seemed she was talking. The physical stress of stardom soon overwhelmed her.

To her horror, a blood vessel near her vocal cords burst, sending her to Nashville's Vanderbilt Hospital for surgery. It was a terrifying experience, and all she could think about was that her career was probably over. After the surgery doctors were optimistic, but they said her throat would have to heal before they would know if it had affected her voice. Their prescription for rehabilitation was simple: She must not speak for two weeks, and after that she would need several months' rest. Her career was put on hold for three months.

To cheer her up, Ted and Edna drove up from Star and brought her plenty of chicken soup and down-home love and affection. But the first two weeks of silence were hard on Faith. Mostly she just lay in bed, big tears streaming down her cheeks. During the past year she had not gone anywhere or done anything without people asking her questions. Talk was a big part of her career—and her life. Now she had to endure thoughts and fears about her career that she could not express, except with pen and paper.

Faith's career had just begun. Was it now over?

The ordeal was equally painful for Scott, who could not bear to see Faith unhappy. One day, while she was still under a "no talking" order from her doctor, Scott told her he had something important to say to her. After expressing his love for her, he showed her an engagement ring and then asked her to marry him.

"Just nod yes or no," he said.

Faith nodded yes.

It Matters to Me

Faith had known Scott for three years when she accepted his marriage proposal. Everyone knew he was deeply in love with her, and throughout 1995 she had told reporters that she was in love with a "special person." This time she was determined to play it by the book—long courtship, engagement . . . then marriage. Everyone had told her she was wrong to give her heart so quickly before. Maybe they had been right. They certainly couldn't say that about her relationship with Scott.

For the first three months of 1995, Faith followed doctor's orders and rested her voice. For someone who was notorious for singing while doing chores, it was sheer torture. Faith was a compulsive singer—always had been, even as a child. The torture was compounded by the fact that she and Scott decided to use her downtime to select songs for her next album. That meant she had to listen to hundreds of demos without injecting her own voice into the mix.

When it came to choosing songs for an album, Faith applied the same test she used when purchasing albums. "As a record-buyer, I don't like hearing a song on the radio and really loving it, going to the record store and buying the album, only to find there's only one or two songs on there

I can listen to," she explained to Alanna Nash. "I've spent twelve or fifteen dollars on something that I won't listen to but one time."

As an artist, Faith looks for songs that will encourage fans to listen to the album from beginning to end. She doesn't listen to a song and then evaluate it as a possible hit. She considers each song as a part of the whole. Of course, that is not the way producers choose songs for an album. They look for hits, songs that have a chance of topping the charts. If the individual songs fit a theme, fine. If they don't, then who cares, really?

Faith and Scott had had an easier time going through songs for her first album. That was partly because she had co-written a number of songs and partly because Scott was in the initial stage of his infatuation with her and was eager to please her. This time around, Faith had no songs of her own to contribute. She had been much too busy touring and doing interviews to spend time with songwriters.

For the first few months, Faith and Scott listened to songs as equal partners. In April 1995 something happened that altered that balance: Scott was named to head Capitol Records' Nashville division, replacing the legendary Jimmy Bowen, who had helped make Garth Brooks into an international star. It was a major appointment and it catapulted Scott into music-industry stardom. Almost overnight he zoomed from the ranks of Nashville's top producers to being the head of the city's most powerful record label.

That created an instant problem with Warner Bros. Scott had gone from being "their" producer, to a position of authority with their biggest competitor. Henceforth their relationship would be as adversaries. And if Warner Bros. dumped Scott as the producer of Faith's next album, then he might pirate her away from them and deliver her to Capitol. He was, after all, more than a producer to Faith. He was going to become her husband.

Scott resolved the dilemma by making a deal with both Warner Bros. and his bosses at Capitol that allowed him to continue to produce Faith's albums. That was unheard-of within the industry—it would be comparable to the chairman of Ford Motors working as a production consultant to General Motors—but neither record label had much choice, not if they wanted a continued association with Scott Hendricks.

At first glance, it seemed like a dream situation for Faith—what recording artist would not want their spouse to be the head of a record label?—but as the weeks went by it became increasingly apparent to Faith that Scott's promotion had fundamentally altered their relationship. No longer were they equals within the industry. No longer was he the man she went to when others pressured her about the direction her artistry would take. He was now the head of a major record label. The song selection on her next album would be viewed by many in Nashville as a test of Scott's abilities as an executive. Her album would now be viewed as a reflection of *his* talents.

The final selection of songs for Faith's second album clearly shows Scott's musical sensibilities and his decision not to stretch her voice to a point where it could permanently injure her vocal cords.

Two songs co-written by Trey Bruce—who had contributed to her debut album—were chosen, "Someone Else's Dream" and "You Can't Lose Me." The former is about a woman who tries to please everyone but herself. Everyone who knew Faith during that time, knows that pleasing other people was her signature in life. Musically, the song did not seem to be in sync with her previous album, but certainly its theme was appropriate.

"Let's Go to Vegas" is about going to Las Vegas to "bet on love and let it ride." Written by Karen Staley, it is an up-tempo number that contains hearty doses of fiddles and piano. It is one of the strongest songs on the album, but it is marred somewhat by Faith's self-conscious effort to make her vocal sound more traditional.

"It Matters to Me" is a lyric-driven ballad about communicating within a relationship. Written by Ed Hill and Mark D. Sanders, the song's most notable musical contribution is a 1980s-style pop guitar riff that transports it beyond the realm of country twang. "A Man's Home Is His Castle," written by Ariel Caton, is a piano-dominant ballad about spousal abuse. Faith half talks, half sings the song, but never really lifts it out of the dungeon.

"Bed of Roses," written by Will Rambeaux and Jaime Kyle, is an up-tempo song that has more clichés than should be legally allowed in one song. "A Room in My Heart," written by Sunny Russ, is a traditional country ballad, while "You Will Be Mine," written by Rob Honey, is another up-tempo song, about a woman who plays by her own rules and considers herself "above the law" when it comes to romance.

While touring with Alan Jackson the previous fall, Jackson had told Faith he wanted to write a song for her. Faith was thrilled at the prospect, but when she eventually received the song it was not what she was looking for, so she told Jackson she would not be able to use it.

Jackson was not used to having his songs rejected, so understandably, it made him angry. But rather than sulk away in defeat, he took another stab at it. The resulting song, "I Can't Do That Anymore," turned out to be one of Faith's favorites on the album. It is about a woman who discovers she needs more out of life than simply sacrificing her needs for her man. The song is hardcore country, with plenty of steel guitar, but it is diminished by the fact that there are times during the song when she sounds identical to Reba.

The highlight of the album is a rafter-lifting gospel tune titled "Keep Walkin' On," written by Karen Staley and Tricia Walker. One of Faith's backup singers, Staley had included the song on an album she released as a solo artist in the 1980s. Faith knew she wanted to use the song the moment she heard it. Its high-energy vocals and rocking piano riff were just the sort of music she'd enjoyed while growing up in Star.

By the time the song selection for the album was complete, Faith was ready to return to the studio. Doctors at the Vanderbilt Voice Center assured her that she had sufficiently recovered to begin singing again—and she carried out her voice exercises with an almost religious intensity—but deep down inside she was fearful that something bad would happen if she turned herself loose.

Scott told her that her voice sounded even better than before, but to her surprise the recording sessions were uneventful. Throughout the album, it was apparent she was being tentative with her vocals. Not helping matters were the songs themselves. None measured up to those on the previous album. Whether that was because of her concerns about her voice, or because Scott pressured her into choosing songs that were more traditional, is unimportant. The album was a good country album, but it offered no possibility of crossover success.

The one song on the album that Faith clearly went to the mat over was "Keep Walkin' On." Recorded with country artist Shelby Lynne, it is the only song on the album where Faith can be heard being herself; it is the only song on the album in which Faith turns loose and allows her vocals to soar.

Shelby Lynne was an unlikely singing partner for Faith. The five-foot-one dynamo of energy had arrived in Nashville in 1986 with high expectations, but by 1995 she was considered a has-been. In nine years she had released four albums on two different labels, but none had spawned that all-important hit.

Scott must have nearly had a heart attack when Faith told him she wanted to do a gospel song with Lynne—by the time Faith recorded "Keep Walkin' On" with her, Lynne was *persona non grata* within the music industry. Part of that had to do with the failure of her albums to top the charts, but it was partly due to the singer's hip appearance and her reputation as a rebel.

Both women were from small towns—Lynne was born in Frankville, Alabama (population 150)—and both thrived on living on the fringes of polite society. There was more to Faith than met the eye. Despite her soft, fluffy exterior, Faith had always pushed life to the edge. She may have appeared soft on the outside, but on the inside she was an adventurous risk-taker.

In Shelby Lynne, Faith saw a kindred spirit, a rebel who didn't care what the gossips said about her. By 1999 Lynne would revive her career with a spectacular rock album titled *I Am Shelby Lynne* (*Details* magazine would label her "hell's belle") but in 1995 she was a music outcast and it was courageous of Faith to take a chance on her.

It was, by any measure, one of the most important years in country-music history. As Faith worked early in 1995 to gather material for her next album, the musical ground beneath her feet was rumbling, a portent of things to come, which would affect her and every singer in country music.

Shania Twain's self-titled 1993 release had disappeared from stores and radio after the release of only two singles, "What Made You Say That" and "Dance with the One that Brought You." Most industry insiders felt Shania had blown her best shot for stardom. Their attitude was, *Who's next?* By the end of 1993 Shania clearly understood it was now or never.

When South African rock producer Robert "Mutt" Lange saw a video of "Dance with the One that Brought You," he instantly became infatuated with the singer and her potential. He was best known for his work with Def Leppard, Michael Bolton, Queen, and Bryan Adams, but he had been a closet country-music fan since childhood. Against his better judgment, he did something totally out of character and called Mercury Records to ask for Shania's telephone number.

Several telephone calls later, Shania and Mutt met for the first time, at the 1993 Fan Fair. He told her he thought she was immensely talented and he wanted to produce her next album, but that it would be important for her to try her hand at writing her own songs. Shania told him she was a prolific songwriter and had turned in a full slate of songs for her first album; unfortunately, all but one of the songs had been rejected by the producers.

Shania and Mutt met with Mercury Records executives and convinced them that they had a plan for the singer's next album, one that would show the world what she could do if given full rein of her talents. Feeling the label had nothing to lose, Mercury Records gave them the go-ahead.

With Shania supplying lyrics, an aggressive postfeminist attitude, and the occasional melody, and Mutt energizing the music with pop-style guitars and the studio techniques that had worked so well with the rock acts he had produced, they created an album unlike anything ever produced in Nashville. They also bonded on a more intimate level and were married before work on the album was completed.

When they turned in the album, they were greeted by polite but stony silence. The record label already had turned down the songs once. What was Shania trying to pull? Only when he listened to the album did Lewis know he had something special. He was mesmerized by the music, but to make certain he played it for the entire staff. Everyone agreed: *The Woman In Me* had the potential to become a hit album.

Shania also made smart use of her obvious sex appeal, according to her manager Mary Bailey. "Up to that point in time, there were no females who had a classy type of sex appeal in conjunction with phenomenal talent," says Bailey. "Dolly [Parton] was the closest, but she used her sex appeal in more of a fun way. She was light and very sensual in a very funny way. . . . Shania is beautiful—let's not kid ourselves—and she is a very sensual woman, but what she brings to the table is that instead of being a threat to the female audience, she is someone they want to be like. She gives them a sense of value and worth."

The Woman In Me, released in February 1995, was not an overnight success. "Whose Bed Have Your Boots Been Under?" was the first single released. Radio's first reaction was one of stunned disbelief. Not only was the music different, offering a "wall of sound" with an energized mix of fiddles and guitars, but the lyrics boasted of a woman who tells her unfaithful man to hit the road; the women in Shania's music world stood by their men, but only if the gesture was reciprocated.

Radio balked, sending word to Mercury Records that Shania was too pop-sounding, too "something" (they weren't sure exactly what) for them to play. The promotions department went to six stations that had aired Shania's first album and begged and pleaded with them to give her a chance. Just let the listeners decide for themselves, they argued. The stations agreed to give it a try. The result was a tidal wave of listener approval. The stations' telephones started ringing and never stopped.

To everyone's surprise, almost all of the callers were women. It was no secret in Nashville that women purchased most of the albums sold in any given year, but never before had they shown much interest in female artists, instead preferring albums recorded by male artists whose sexuality figured prominently into the equation.

Of course, country music has a long history of female entertainers—Dolly Parton, Reba McEntire, Tammy Wynette, to name a few—but never had they sold records in huge numbers. They were second-class citizens of the music world in every sense. Shania Twain changed all that—and in a meaningful way. Not only did she show leadership in sales, she showed it politically, by the way in which she took charge of her career and produced music that had a clearly defined gender bias.

In the decades before the success of Shania Twain, women had worked their way up the corporate ladder, moving from receptionist to executive assistant to media-relations director, but none was really in a position to capitalize on it in a gender-friendly way—that is, until Shania proved that women could sell records.

Within weeks of its release, *The Woman In Me* topped the country charts, and by September 1995 it had peaked at number 6 on the pop charts, as well. Its first year out, it sold more than twelve million copies, making it the best-selling album ever recorded by a female country artist. By 2000, it had sold over seventeen million copies, making Shania Twain the biggest-selling country-music artist, male or female, in history.

To the shock of everyone, including her own record label, Shania refused to go out on tour to support the album. Her reasoning was that she simply didn't have enough songs to fill a concert set. Mercury Records pleaded with her to change her mind, to no avail.

Concert promoters, radio program directors, the sales staff at the record label, all thought it was a mistake. They had never heard of a woman calling the shots on whether she would tour or not. It all seemed like something out of a bad dream.

In August 1995, *Entertainment Weekly* published a story titled "Babes in Opryland" that attempted to deal with the gender politics of country music. "Shania Twain, the Canadian rookie with a voice modeled after Linda Ronstadt's and a video presence à la Cindy Crawford, is now achieving Top Ten pop-crossover success," wrote Ken Tucker. "Given these contrasting examples of brash showmanship, low-key authenticity, and hubba-hubba slinkiness, what's a girl to do?"

The article featured photographs of Terri Clark, Carlene Carter, and Helen Darling, along with reviews of their albums, but Shania was mentioned only in passing and Faith Hill was totally ignored, despite the success of her debut album. In a second article in the same issue of *Entertainment Weekly*, Shania was asked if her good looks had anything to do with her success. Her response was to the point: "Marilyn Monroe never sold a platinum album."

In early 1996, *The Hollywood Reporter* published a country-music special issue titled, "Women Rule: With the men sounding more and more alike, country's female stars are leading the way." The magazine did interviews with Trisha Yearwood, Deana Carter, Patty Loveless, and others, but managed to mention Faith Hill only in passing.

Interviewed by Alan Waldman for the article was new Capitol Records boss Scott Hendricks, who promoted his label's two emerging stars, Trace Adkins and Deana Carter, whose debut album *Did I Shave My Legs for This?* created a stir with its irreverent take on 1990s sexuality. "Trace and Deana broke through because they don't sound like anybody else, but the labels are also bringing out a lot of clones," said Hendricks. "Some of them may be good, but they sound a lot like somebody we've already got."

Faith Hill was delighted by Shania's success, for she saw the Canadian singer as a pioneer who kicked down the door for all female country artists—in later years she would publicly thank Shania for what she has done for women—but Faith must have been baffled by Scott's attitude toward her as an artist.

At the same time that Scott was applauding the boldness of Capitol Records artist Deana Carter, he was urging Faith to become more traditional in her approach to music. Was he doing that because Faith would soon become his wife and he felt protective? Or was he doing it because he no longer felt she could be competitive with the Shania Twains and Deana Carters of the world?

Shania Twain's success did more than encourage Faith to reevaluate the direction her music was taking. It prompted her to reevaluate her personal relationships, both in and out of the studio.

Warner Bros. could not possibly have picked a worse time to release Faith's second album, *It Matters to Me*. Radio and music fans alike were clamoring for more records that offered the feisty sex appeal of artists such as Shania Twain and Deana Carter. Twang was out and "hot mama" was in.

Although the first single, "It Matters to Me," went to number one on the country charts not long after its release—and the album sold over half a million copies its first year—it never crossed over to tap the pop market that had proved so friendly to Twain and Carter. The three singles that followed ("Let's Go to Vegas," "You Can't Lose Me," and "I Can't Do That Anymore") fared no better with the pop charts.

The fact that so much of the album sounded like something that Reba McEntire might record, hurt Faith in more ways than one. When Faith had been a teenager in the 1980s, Reba was one of the hottest acts on the concert tour, but by 1995 the redheaded singer was out of touch with the new wave of music sweeping Nashville. Inviting comparisons to Reba was the *last* thing Faith should have done to further her own career.

The same year Faith's album was released, Reba decided to relocate her own offices from the fairgrounds to a new three-story building on Music Row. Everyone thought that was just fine, until Reba announced plans to build a helicopter pad on the roof of the building. The very thought of noisy helicopters swooping down on the historic tranquility of Music Row got the ole boys out on the street kicking up their boots in outrage. The confrontation was headed toward the city council and a possible court case, when Reba reluctantly backed down and put her plans on hold.

To the outside world Reba was a music legend, someone to be admired and respected. But many people within the industry considered her a troublemaker, a fading star whose musical style was a thing of the past.

Faith seemed oblivious to the implications of all that. Not only was Reba her childhood hero, Reba was someone to be admired for the way she dealt with her fans. "I think the compassion that she has for people is real," Faith explained to Alanna Nash. "She has a real compassion not only with her employees, when something's really wrong, but with her fans. When fans come up and you know they're really so nervous they can hardly stand it, they're shaking, but Reba has this way of making them feel so comfortable that they leave there and they're not nervous anymore. . . . She has this gift of making that person, at that point, feel like they are the only person in that room."

Faith's personal relationship with husband-to-be Scott Hendricks must have suffered during this time. Scott was not only her fiancé, he was her record producer. How could he be so wrong about *It Matters to Me* and so right about Deana Carter's *Did I Shave My Legs for This?* How could he encourage Faith to pull back on her sexuality, when the entire city was headed toward a more risqué image for female artists?

Faith wouldn't have been human if she were not confused about their relationship. Clearly she and Scott had differing opinions about the place of sexuality in the music business, for her appearance changed drastically in the fall of 1995. The tabloids reported that Faith underwent breast augmentation, increasing her bust from a size 36B to 36C, and even though she has always denied it, she did present a decidedly bustier appearance.

On top of everything else, Scott was having a difficult time dealing with Capitol Records' most successful artist, Garth Brooks. Everyone naturally had assumed that they would be the best of friends. They both grew up in Oklahoma, no more than fifty miles apart, their high schools played against each other, and they both attended Oklahoma State University in Stillwater. If that wasn't a basis for friendship in a town that was increasingly becoming a melting pot of radically differing cultures, what would be?

What Scott found when he took over the reins at Capitol was a company that was "Garthing" its way out of business. Garth's lucrative royalty contract made it difficult for the company to make money. Scott's first assignment was to clamp down on Garth and to exert his authority as the head of the record label.

Garth went into his relationship with Scott with an open mind. He had been unhappy with the way Jimmy Bowen ran the record label, so he had to think Scott had nowhere to go but up. That's not what happened. During one of their first meetings, Scott attempted to assure Garth of his respect for his music, only it didn't sound that way to Garth. "You know, Garth, if your shit stinks, I'm gonna tell you," Scott told the singer, according to author Laurence Leamer. Garth didn't like the sound of that at all. He took it to be an insult, and possibly a threat. "I don't believe in you guys," Garth responded. "And from what I understand, you guys are not very good."

Scott could have ended the conflict on the spot by stroking Garth's ego, but he chose not to, perhaps thinking that "tough love" was the best way to handle Garth.

From all appearances, Scott's reactions to Faith and her career were characterized by a similar approach. Garth and Faith share a distinction in character. They both have forgiving hearts, but when it comes to confrontations over misdeeds or miscalculations, they offer only one chance to make amends. If you don't say you are sorry—and mean it—they head for the door and never look back.

Scott failed to acknowledge to Garth that he made a mistake, thus dooming his tenure at Capitol Records, and he failed to take responsibility for his miscalculation on Faith's latest album, killing any chance he had of getting her to walk down the aisle with him (they had been engaged for months, but Faith resisted any attempt to set a wedding date). As a commercial record producer, Scott was as good as they come, but as a communicator he had a great deal to learn.

Faith is a person who speaks through her emotions—her first refuge is always in tears—and through her actions—where her last refuge is usually in the badlands of defiant behavior. Her outlaw streak emerged at the 1995 Country Music Association Awards, when she performed "Keep Walkin' On" with Shelby Lynne. For her to sing a gospel song, and not one of the songs earmarked as singles from her album, was tantamount to thumbing her nose at the establishment. Simply being onstage with Lynne made the gossips livid. Faith did not receive an ACM or CMA award that year, but she did receive a TNN/*Music City News* award as the female "Star of Tomorrow."

⟿ Faith was lucky that she had a new album to promote. That meant she could hit the road and leave all her Nashville worries behind. As luck would have it, the headliner for her tour was Alan Jackson. Ordinarily that would be a good thing, but the latter part of 1995 and early 1996 was turning out to be a very bad time in his life. His marriage was beginning to show signs of strain (he would separate from his wife, Denise, for three months in 1998) and hit records were becoming harder to make. His 1996 hit, "Little Bitty," would be the last he would have until the new millennium. He didn't like what was happening with country music, and he was vocal in his opposition to the genre's rising infatuation with power ballads and pop-heavy rock rhythms. He liked his music raw, stripped down to its big-twang essentials.

Faith also was the opening act for a number of concerts with Reba McEntire during this time. While she considered Jackson a superstar and Reba a living legend, she could not have chosen two worse acts to travel with, at least from a public-relations standpoint. Without mentioning any particular female artist by name, Jackson complained about what the new pop-sounding music was doing to traditional country music. His comments, by association, reflected badly on Faith. Likewise, by appearing on the same stage with Reba, it confirmed the suspicions of some that Faith aspired to become a Reba clone.

Faith usually enjoyed being out on the road, but this time there seemed to be a lot of technical problems and tensions within the band. Equipment failures and musical miscues are never much fun, even during the best of times, but out on the road they can be nerve-wracking. "I'm scared for my life the moment I walk onstage," Faith told *Country Music* magazine. When things got really crazy, Faith's antidote was to have the bus driver pull over at a roadside market so she could purchase fresh vegetables to cook for herself and her band.

One of the highlights of 1995 for Faith was a trip with Scott, Reba, and Reba's husband Narvel Blackstock to Dallas, where Reba sang the National Anthem at a Dallas Cowboys–San Francisco 49ers game. The sold-out stadium went wild for Reba, confirming for Faith the validity of using the singer as a role model for her own career.

On the plane ride back to Nashville, according to author Laurence Leamer, Reba fell into one of her "talking moods" in which she recalled the stresses of her first marriage. Was she being reflective about her own life or was she responding to what her intuition told her were difficulties in Faith's relationship with Scott?

Whatever her intent, Scott took Reba's words as affirmation of the strength of his relationship with Faith. "[Reba] had her own jet planes, a loving husband, and the biggest career of any woman in country music," observed Leamer. "It was just possible that you could have it all, just possible, Reba and Narvel, Faith and Scott."

That Christmas, Scott, who was as much in love as a man could be, basked in the radiant glow of his bride-to-be as Faith prepared for her upcoming concert tour with the bad boy of country music, Tim McGraw.

Love Is a Sweet Thing

In March 1994, Tim McGraw's "Indian Outlaw" was the hottest country single on the charts since Billy Ray Cyrus's 1992 chart-buster, "Achy Breaky Heart." You would think that would be good news, but there was a problem: Radio stations balked at playing the record after Native American organizations protested that it was racist.

One state that was especially troublesome was Minnesota, where two radio stations yanked the song from their playlists. WaBunn-Inini, president of the Minneapolis-based National Coalition of Racism in Sports and the Media (these are the same folks that protested about Atlanta Braves fans making a tomahawk-chop gesture during the games), told the *Los Angeles Times* that "people up here are really upset. . . . It's cheap Hollywood music like the tomahawk-chop chant or the old Hamm's beer song."

Tim was stunned by the criticism, but refused to repudiate the song. "You're concerned anytime somebody doesn't like something you do, but you're never going to please everybody," the twenty-six-year-old singer told the *Los Angeles Times*. "A lot of times a song or something like the 'tomahawk-chop' isn't the real issue, but a means to an ends, a way to be heard."

Nothing stirs up curiosity about a recording artist in Nashville faster than a little controversy on the subject of racism, however misleading or wrongheaded the controversy may be. That's because the city is hyper-sensitive to racial issues because of the unfortunate things that happened during the civil-rights era, and because the country-music industry has expended a great deal of effort and money fending off the redneck imagery sometimes associated with its product.

Tim McGraw was branded an outlaw from the get-go, exactly the type of bad boy mothers advise their daughters not to associate with. The questions on everyone's lips were "Who is this guy?" and "Where did he come from?"

⟿ Tim's road to Nashville was rocky at best. It all began in late summer 1966 at an apartment complex in Jacksonville, Florida, where Tim's mother-to-be, Elizabeth Ann Dagostino (she prefers to be called Betty), lived with her mother and sister. Her parents were divorced. Betty was eighteen at the time and not sure what she wanted to do with her life.

Living downstairs from her was a twenty-two-year-old baseball pitcher for the Jacksonville Suns. His name was Frank McGraw, but everyone called him "Tug." Betty and Tug were acquainted, but they did not get involved in an intimate relationship, as she explained in her book *Tim McGraw: A Mother's Story*, until the day she had an argument with her mother and then went downstairs to visit Tug in his apartment. They had unprotected sex, and when she left, she was on her way to becoming a mother.

Not long after she found out she was pregnant, her mother and father reunited and moved the family to Delhi, Louisiana. The entire family was upset over Betty's pregnancy and urged her to get in touch with Tug to see if he would do the right thing. By that time Tug had moved to New York, where he had been signed by the Mets. According to Betty, he declined to get involved with her pregnancy.

On May 1, 1967, Samuel Timothy McGraw was born at a clinic in Delhi, Louisiana. Although still a teenager, Betty decided to keep her son and raise him herself with her family's support. That proved more difficult when her mother and father separated again, this time for good. Betty and little Timmy followed her mother, first to Rayville, Louisiana, where Betty found a job as a waitress in a truck stop, then later to the larger city of Monroe. When an older man named Horace Smith offered to marry her and be a father to little Timmy, Betty, realizing she was quickly running out of options, readily agreed. Within months Betty was pregnant again, giving birth to a daughter, Tracey, in September 1968. By April 1971 she had a second daughter, named Sandy.

Growing up, Tim had two passions—music and sports. His first public singing experience occurred in church, where at the age of three he stood to sing "Jesus Loves Me." His interest in sports was realized with Little League baseball.

By the time Tim was nine, Betty filed for divorce. Tim continued to consider Horace Smith his father until the age of eleven, when he came across his birth certificate while looking for a photograph. The certificate named Frank (Tug) McGraw as his dad. "I was like any kid would be," Tim told *People* magazine. "At first, it's wow, your dad's a pro baseball player. Then, of course, that wears off."

One year later, Betty succeeded in arranging a meeting between Tim and his father when Tug's team, the Philadelphia Phillies, traveled to Houston to play the Astros. Tug was friendly and polite, but nothing developed in the way of a relationship until Tim's senior year of high school, when they met for a second time, at Betty's insistence. This time Betty suggested that Tug help their son with his college education. Tug agreed to pay for Tim's education at a four-year college. Despite the focus on money issues, they were able to bond as father and son. Both realized at that point that if they were to have an adult relationship it would have to be based on the future and not the past.

After graduating from Monroe Christian High School in 1985, Tim turned down a baseball scholarship to enroll at Northeast Louisiana University. While there, Tim did what many college students do to help pass the time, he bought a twenty-dollar guitar in a pawnshop. He taught himself to play guitar and he watched enough music videos on television to learn the words of the songs then on the charts. Before long, he attracted the attention of a Monroe talent promoter, Carol McCoy, who worked with him to develop his talent. "He was a diamond in the rough," she told writer Roger Hitts. "I had managed better singers, but Tim had it all to be a superstar. He didn't believe me, so I had to take time and care developing him."

By 1989 Tim had had enough of college, where he was not proving himself to be the best of students anyway, and he struck out to Nashville to form a honky-tonk band. For two long years, he and his band performed whenever and wherever they could. The band members supplemented their income by purchasing silk roses and reselling them to the women in the nightclubs where they performed. On a good night, the women tossed the roses onstage to Tim, where they were later gathered up by the band and resold the next night.

Finally, with the help of Tug, who knew someone who knew someone, Tim landed a recording contract in 1991 with Curb Records. It was an odd pairing in many respects. Tim was rough around the edges, hardened somewhat by his nightly experiences in honky-tonks and dives all over the city. He looked and acted like a tough guy, though he was always respectful toward authority figures, just as he had been taught to do by his mother.

Mike Curb, the founder of Curb Records, lived in a world that was light-years apart from the one Tim knew and understood. The son of an FBI agent and the grandson of a Baptist preacher, Curb is a George Bush–style Republican who entered the music business in the late 1960s as the leader of the Mick Curb Congregation, a singing group that performed often on *The Glen Campbell Goodtime Hour*.

At the age of twenty, he had formed a record company, Sidewalk Records, which he later merged with cash-hungry MGM Records. By 1969, Curb was the president of MGM. To the dismay of many in the industry, he publicly took a stand against illegal drugs and promised to release from contract any act that advocated drug use as a lifestyle issue. Frank Zappa was his first casualty.

Over the next several years, Curb parlayed his conservatism into a string of hit records, including the Osmonds' first hit, "One Bad Apple" and Debby Boone's "You Light Up My Life." He also showed an interest in Republican politics. In 1976 he was chairman of Ronald Reagan's presidential campaign in California. Two years later, he ran for lieutenant governor of California—and won. One of his duties was to serve as acting governor when Governor Jerry Brown was out of the state (which was often).

When Curb moved to Nashville in the early 1990s with his wife and daughters, he was a decided curiosity: Not only was he the only Republican former lieutenant governor to work on Music Row, he was the wealthiest music executive in town, with an estimated personal wealth of $50 million to $100 million, according to *Business Nashville*.

There is no dispute on Music Row about Curb's instincts—he signed the Judds to their first contract, and he signed LeAnn Rimes when other labels thought she was too young—but there has been talk over the years that he has allowed his Republican business instincts take priority over his artists' interests, something he vociferously denies. "There's a lot more competition in this town than I expected when I moved here," he told *Nashville Scene* writer Beverly Keel. "It's not one big happy family. It's a very competitive town where all the major labels, with the exception of mine, are owned by big companies, and there's a lot of pressure."

This, then, was the man to whom Tim McGraw relinquished his musical soul. Just seeing Mike Curb and Tim McGraw in the same room together would be worth the price of a ticket, and his signing certainly generated interest on Music Row. Everyone figured that Mike Curb must have a plan—and he did.

Tim's debut album, released in 1992, disappeared off the charts almost immediately. But his second album, *Not a Moment Too Soon*, was a major hit in 1994, selling more than five million copies, despite the controversy associated with its bestselling single, "Indian Outlaw." One of the reasons for the album's success was the second single, the heart-tugging "Don't Take the Girl," a ballad that established Tim as a major star, and a heartthrob to millions of female CD-buyers.

The key to Tim's success was the crossover appeal of his music, and that was a formula that Mike Curb knew something about. It was, in fact, the key to his success with artists such as the Osmonds, Debby Boone, and the Judds. "Historically, a lot of artists have been crossed both ways in pop and country, but when I moved to Nashville, I was told that you weren't supposed to cross records, you'll offend country radio," he told Darryl Morden of *The Hollywood Reporter*. "I wish someone would've told me; I've been crossing records for thirty years."

Curb clearly had seen something in Tim's rough exterior, something he could gloss over and present to country radio. Whatever the philosophy at work, Tim was grateful. "I'm thankful for Mike Curb's faithful interest in my career," Tim told the trade magazine. "[He] has believed in my music and given me the freedom to record the kind of music I want to produce."

The following year Tim released *All I Want*, his third album on Curb Records. The first single, "I Like It, I Love It," spent five weeks at number one, and the second single, "Can't Really Be Gone," went to the top spot only eight weeks after its release.

As Tim entered 1996, it was shaping up to be his biggest year ever. He had everything a man would want: fame, money, the respect of his peers. He had everything—except a woman to love.

⟶ Faith began 1996 filled with doubts. Her most recent album, *It Matters to Me*, was selling well, but it wasn't doing much to advance her career. Faith had been in Nashville for nine years—nine long years!—and nothing was happening the way she had hoped and dreamed. It wasn't just the music, either. It had been over nine months since Scott had proposed to her, and she was reluctant to set a wedding date. Luckily for her, tour dates kept popping up, allowing her to make excuses to hit the road.

It was during that downtime after Christmas that Tim McGraw's manager called and asked if Faith would be interested in opening for Tim on his spring and summer tour. Faith jumped at the chance and agreed to a meeting with Tim at one of his shows.

Faith had met Tim at the 1994 Country Radio Seminar, but they were both novices at that point and he didn't seem like someone it would be important for her to know, so he hadn't made much of an impression. That wasn't the case with Tim though, who had been smitten by her beauty and easygoing Southern charm. They'd met again in 1995 when their tours intersected in Wisconsin, but Tim considered her way out of his league and he didn't pursue her, especially since she showed no interest in him.

It was not until they met to discuss the tour that Faith saw Tim in a different light. "I was really attracted to him," she told VH1. "I mean, he's very sexy. I thought he was, just from rumors that he was this tough guy, dark and tough, but he's not like that at all."

The best thing Tim had going was that he was the opposite of Scott in almost every way. Scott was methodical, mindful of the politics of his decisions; Tim was reckless, unconcerned about what other people thought. Scott was masculine enough, but he was more the quiet, James Stewart type; Tim's masculinity was derived more from his muscular, athletic build and his Sean Penn–like volatility. Scott wanted to marry her and control her career; Tim had no thoughts about her career—he wanted her the way a man traditionally wants a woman, to hell with the paperwork.

Tim's 1996 outing was named the "Spontaneous Combustion" tour. It was all that, and more. Not long after the tour kicked off on March 14 in Wheeling, West Virginia, sparks were flying between the two performers. Tim made the first move by inviting Faith to his dressing room after one of their shows. As soon as she entered the room, he embraced her and kissed her on the mouth—a firm, lingering kiss that informed her of his intentions. Faith was shocked, but not offended.

"I was only with him for a couple of days and I fell madly in love with him," she told VH1. "I mean, he was just like a magnet. It was like, I have to be with this man for the rest of my life. Period. As simple as that."

The affair began innocently enough with stolen kisses—and shared dinners and movies, the things that high-school kids do—but it soon progressed, so that within weeks of the tour's start, rumors began floating back to Nashville about the two of them. The pair performed a duet that became more and more passionate each night. Soon it got to the point where they ended the song with a kiss.

Scott had heard rumors before about Faith, but always they had turned out to be nothing more than vicious, backstabbing attempts to cause Faith pain. He believed in her, and he believed in their relationship. He assumed that Tim would call him the same way Troy Aikman had done, to assure him that he had nothing to worry about.

That telephone call from Tim never came.

Later, talking to reporters, Tim was honest about his game plan. "I used my power as the headliner to make sure she fell in love with me," he joked to Josh Rottenberg of *US Weekly*, although there was probably a lot of truth in his statement. More to the point, he said: "You can't meet Faith and not fall in love with her. I just got lucky. The first time I saw her walk onto the stage and start singing, I was just mesmerized by her."

Why would they *not* fall in love?

Aside from a mutual physical attraction that had all the sizzle of an R-rated Hollywood movie, there were other, more important elements at work in their relationship. For Faith it was the fact that Tim's mother had kept him and raised him, despite the hardships involved. He was an example of what could happen if mothers did not abandon their children. Faith had made peace with her birth mother, but the circumstances of her birth still haunted her, still made her feel as if she were somehow on the outside looking in.

Tim's attraction to Faith had many of the same psychosocial ingredients. Tim had abandonment issues with his father and trust issues with his mother for not telling him the truth about his birth until he was eleven years of age. When Faith poured her heart out about her situation, Tim knew exactly how she felt. He didn't tell her to get over it, the way her first husband apparently had. And he didn't ignore it, the way Scott apparently did. That is not to say that Scott and Daniel were wrong—it was simply a life experience beyond their everyday range of emotions. Tim shared her pain, and that was what made him indispensable to her. People could gossip all they wanted, Faith and Tim had found their soul mates and that was all that was important to them.

During one of their layovers in Nashville, Faith broke it off with Scott. It could not have come at a worse time for him. Garth Brooks was fighting him for control of Capitol Records, and he was losing (by May he would be replaced at the record label by Pat Quigley, Garth's personal choice). Scott was devastated by the breakup with Faith, and to this day he will not discuss it with the media.

Faith was more philosophical. "It obviously wasn't a rock-solid situation or it wouldn't have ended," she told Jim Jerome of *People* magazine. "If someone is going to judge my character because I was engaged to somebody and then I left him for somebody else—'Oh, okay, now she's a slut and a bad person'—I can't control that. But I wasn't about to let Tim slip through my hands. And I had more self-worth and self-respect to not stay in a situation just because someone else thinks I should. I have to be happy, too."

This business of how to behave in relationships was something Faith had given a lot of thought to after her divorce. "Even though people around you are telling you things, it doesn't matter," she told Alanna Nash in 1995. "Nobody knows you like you know you. And it takes awhile for me to know that, because I want to always do the right thing. But, you know, it's okay if I don't always do the right thing. It doesn't mean that I'm a bad person. Everybody makes mistakes. If you didn't, how could you possibly grow?" That was always at the core of Faith's evaluation of a relationship: whether it allowed for growth or stifled it by making her feel guilty for wanting to spread her wings.

As far as Nashville was concerned, Tim was the outlaw, the white-trash interloper who yearned for a touch of class and respectability, and Faith was the elegant blonde belle who yearned to be an ass-kicking outlaw. Typically, with its ear to the ground to any variation of the love-gone-wrong or -right theme, Nashville was correct on both accounts. Tim and Faith were opposites who wanted to become the same.

Despite their passion for each other, they never verbalized it until August, when they went for a Jeep ride in the Pennsylvania countryside. Faith wore a denim jacket and jeans, a navy cap, and dark sunglasses. Tim wore a red sweater and jeans, with a light blue cap and matching sunglasses. Clearly they had made themselves up to enjoy their time together incognito, away from the prying eyes of the public.

At one point Tim pulled off the road and stopped the Jeep.

"Okay, is this for real?"

Faith assured him it was for real.

From that point on, they knew they would become a couple.

The summer and fall of 1996 was a golden one for both of them. Tim's new single from his *All I Want* album, "She Never Lets It Go to Her Heart," went to number one and guaranteed sold-out concerts across the country. By the time it ended, it would be one of the top five grossing tours of the year.

Faith was getting no action from her last album, but other things were happening in her life. That year, with the help of Warner Bros. Records and Time-Warner, she launched the Faith Hill Family Literacy Project, a program designed to help combat illiteracy worldwide. She had a personal interest in the project because of her father's inability to read. It was too late to help her father, but maybe it was not too late for others like him. Said Faith: "Someday every person will be able to read."

Also that summer, Faith was asked to perform in the closing ceremonies of the 1996 Summer Olympics in Atlanta. It was one of the most nerve-wracking bookings of her career. Everyone was on edge because of the July 27 bombing that took place in Centennial Park. The blast killed a Georgia woman, caused the fatal heart attack of a Turkish photographer, and injured over one hundred revelers. Authorities could not guarantee that it would not happen again.

Performing that August evening, less than one week after the bombing, were Stevie Wonder, who sang John Lennon's "Imagine" as the crowd of eighty thousand stood and swayed to the music and an estimated audience of three and a half *billion* viewers sat before their television sets, Gloria Estefan and her energetic Miami Sound Machine, numerous marching bands, and others. Faith did her part, although she never looked truly relaxed during her performance.

Billy Payne, president of the Atlanta Committee for the Olympic Games, seemed relieved to make it through the contests without further violence. "While we will always remember in our hearts the loss, the reclaiming of our city, the defiance the entire Olympic family showed, is a more powerful story that will ultimately be the way the Games are remembered."

Faith would remember the Olympic Games for other reasons, for it was within weeks of her performance that the couple first talked about marriage. It happened at a concert venue in Montana. Before going on-stage, Tim and Faith relaxed in a trailer house that had been installed at the venue for the comfort of the performers. Tim, never one to waste time, said it flat out: "I want you to marry me."

Faith's first response was that she could not believe he would ask her that question in a house trailer. Tim stood his ground. What do you expect, he said—we're country singers! Faith asked for time to make up her mind. While he was onstage, Faith wrote her answer with a Sharpie on a mirror: *I'm going to be your wife. Yes, F.* Tim reciprocated with a five-carat canary-yellow diamond ring set in gold.

They did not want to wait too long to get married; the sooner, the better. They decided to exchange vows on October 6 in Tim's hometown of Rayville, Louisiana, where he did a benefit performance each year to help raise money for scholarships and athletic facilities. They invited friends and family to attend the event, but did not tell them that they planned to be married. As a result, everyone showed up in shorts, T-shirts, and jeans, dressed for what they thought would be a softball game.

Faith, wearing a white dress and standing barefoot, and Tim, dressed in jeans and a long black coat, stood beneath the shade of an oak tree at high noon and exchanged vows before a minister who quickly pronounced them "man and wife."

When they returned to Nashville, they were treated like royalty. Not since George Jones and Tammy Wynette had such a high-profile music couple tied the knot. The last concert of the Spontaneous Combustion tour was given on New Year's Eve at the Nashville downtown arena, where Tim and Faith displayed their affection for each other onstage, sending a clear message for all to see, that the outlaw and the angel were now a team to be reckoned with.

The highlight of the evening occurred when the couple sang a duet, a song that had not yet been recorded—"It's Your Love," written by former Memphis songwriter Stephony Smith. The audience went wild. Faith and Tim could have received another, even bigger, round of applause if they had told the audience their secret: Faith was pregnant.

CHAPTER 7

There Will Come a Day

Exhausted not just from the physical demands of the tour, but also from her pregnancy, Faith began 1997 with a decision to take most of the year off so that she could devote more time to herself and her family. That was fine with Tim, who looked forward to having his new bride all to himself. Except for recording a new album, he, too, planned to take time off during the first half of the year.

As Scott Hendricks licked his wounds—and Warner Bros. wondered when Faith would be ready to return to the studio—the happy couple settled into their four-bedroom colonial home in Brentwood (an upscale suburb of Nashville) and played house, behaving much like teenagers who had been left in charge by their parents.

The hiatus gave Faith an opportunity to listen to music again for the first time in a long while. The past year of her life had been so hectic there had been no time to replenish her soul with the music that was important to her. "There was a point where I was so busy working and so tired and burnt-out a bit that I would never put CDs on—and I love music," she told *TV Guide*. "So it was hard to get inspired to go to the next phase in my career."

Professionally, Tim was in the best—and worst—of worlds. He had just ended his best year yet, with a successful tour and a hit album, but now it was time to do it all over again. What if he couldn't duplicate that success? What if 1996 was destined to be his *only* good year? Added to those doubts was the pressure he felt as a husband and father-to-be. For the first time in his life he found himself in a position where he had to take into consideration the needs of others.

Recording artists who write their own songs tend to envision albums as collections of disparate elements that share a common vision or theme. Artists who don't write their own songs can sometimes accomplish that same goal by searching for songs that share similarities of style or theme, but it requires a little more work.

For his songs, Tim relies almost entirely on the production team put together by producer Byron Gallimore. They wade through hundreds of songs, some written specifically for Tim, others written for no particular artist, and they narrow the choices down to a manageable number. Tim and Gallimore go through that list to find the dozen or so songs that will actually be on the album.

"A lot of songs we find aren't necessarily new songs—sometimes they are ones that have been around for a while," Tim told country.com. "I'm always looking for something a little different. We dig deep to find the material, and I try to find songs that fit me. I have passed on hits, but they are hits for other singers, not me."

When he started work on *Everywhere*, his fourth album for Curb Records, he knew the title of one song that would make the album—"It's Your Love," the song he and Faith had performed together at the New Year's Eve concert. It was a duet in the loosest sense of the term, since Faith's contribution was to provide background vocals that blend with his lead vocal, but her presence in the song was strong nonetheless.

The album contained eleven songs including the title track, "Where the Green Grass Grows," "For a Little While," and "You Just Get Better All the Time." Not until after all the vocals had been recorded was Faith asked to come in to sing her part on "It's Your Love." Her child was due any day at that point and it required real effort on her part to sing, primarily because of the way her extra weight affected her breathing, but she performed beautifully, giving Tim and Gallimore exactly what they wanted.

When she left the studio, Tim and Gallimore were speechless. There was something magical about Faith, even to the man who saw her each day without makeup and in curlers. Sometimes artists know they have a hit when they hear it for the first time on playback. That was the case with "It's Your Love." It sounded like a sure thing.

⌐ On May 5, 1997, seven months after Tim and Faith's marriage, Gracie Katherine McGraw came into the world at Nashville's Baptist Hospital. Also in the hospital that day was pop star Peter Cetera, there to attend the birth of his daughter, Sena.

When Faith left the hospital with Gracie in her arms, she felt vaguely guilty, as if she were getting away with something illegal, like stealing a candy bar or playing chicken with a speeding locomotive. She told friends it was the happiest day of her life.

"Becoming a parent changes everything," she told the *Kansas City Star*. "Having children has inspired me in every area of my life and certainly that's true of me as an artist. I love my music, but in a way it has become less important because it's not the only thing in my life. You look at music differently after you have a child."

For the next five or six months, Faith stayed at home, devoting all her efforts to the care of her newborn baby. Finally she had the life she had dreamed about. Despite the success of her first two albums, she had felt unfulfilled in her personal life. Scott was a great guy, who had loved her with all his heart, but she had never felt secure in the relationship; there was always something missing. Not until she met Tim did she see herself as both a wife and a performer.

There was excitement in her eyes all summer. She experienced emotions she had only heard and read about. People sometimes live a lifetime without ever experiencing the joys of motherhood and a loving marital relationship. It gave Faith a confidence she had never had. Just the thought of it was enough to bring her to tears.

Tim was equally emotional about their relationship, telling *People* magazine the best part of his day was simply lying in bed late at night with Faith and Gracie asleep at his side: "I flip through the channels and keep looking over at them sleeping. They're just, like, cuddled up right next to each other."

At the end of the summer, Faith left her idyllic life in Brentwood to attend the Thirty-first Annual Country Music Association Awards show on September 24, 1997. It was Faith's first personal appearance since she had given birth to Gracie and it probably would not have occurred but for the fact that she and Tim were nominated for their duet on his hit song "It's Your Love."

Tim had been out and about for months, promoting his new album, particularly the duet, which remained at or near the top of the charts for most of the year. His outings were not on the level of the heralded Spontaneous Combustion tour, but according to *Performance* magazine, he grossed more than $3 million for the year.

To no one's surprise, Faith and Tim won the award for Vocal Event of the Year for their recording of "It's Your Love." It was Faith's first CMA award. "All of us sit when we're younger and watch the show, and hope we'll have the opportunity to stand up here and give an acceptance speech and hold one of these awards," Faith told Tom Roland of the Nashville *Tennessean*. "It makes it one million times better to win this award with my husband."

Other winners included fellow Mississippian LeAnn Rimes, who took home the Horizon Award; Trisha Yearwood, for Female Vocalist of the Year; Brooks and Dunn in the Vocal Duo category; Kathy Mattea for Video of the Year; and Garth Brooks, for Entertainer of the Year.

By far the biggest excitement of the evening occurred when the Song of the Year award was announced by presenter Ricky Skaggs. The winner was Deana Carter's "Strawberry Wine." Upon hearing her name, the barefoot Carter dashed across the stage and leaped into Skagg's arms, squeezing him tightly about the neck and wrapping her legs about his waist. The startled Skaggs looked at the audience in disbelief.

"I was just floored," she later said in a press conference. "I almost did a handspring. It's been awhile, but I was going to give it a shot, and I apologize to Ricky Skaggs, too. I certainly didn't mean to insult his wife like that. I was just excited about it."

〜 Over the past two years, country music had undergone a major overhaul. By 1997 and 1998, Shania Twain's success had propelled women to the forefront. Women were *everywhere*—at the top of the charts, in the studios, in the executive offices, in the promotion and publicity offices. They were producing their own albums, writing their own songs, and playing their own instruments. And if they occasionally displayed a little affectionate wildness during normally-staid awards ceremonies, so be it—certainly they had earned the right to let down their hair and whoop it up every once in a while.

Deana Carter was one of the more playful new artists on the scene. That may have been because she grew up in a musical household. Her father, Fred Carter Jr., was a well-known session guitarist in Nashville who had played with many of the headliners of the 1960s and 1970s: Roy Orbison, Willie Nelson, Waylon Jennings, Bob Dylan, to name a few. When Deana heard stories about those people at the dinner table, they were more than legends, they were real people who sometimes engaged in funny, unpredictable, and outlandish behavior; that was what *she* wanted to do when she grew up.

By the age of seventeen, she knew what she wanted most in life was a career in music. She talked her father into taking her by the studios and record labels to introduce her to all the right people. She figured that if the important people could meet her, see her eyeball-to-eyeball, they would recognize her inherent talent and offer her a record deal. Everyone was happy to meet her, of course—they all had heard the stories about how Fred had once written a song for Dean Martin and had named his daughter after the crooner—but that was as far as it went. They didn't just give record contracts to people they liked. On the contrary, the contracts usually went to people they despised.

When no one showed any interest in her as a recording artist, she entered the University of Tennessee to study rehabilitation therapy. After graduation she worked with stroke and head-injury patients in recovery for a couple of years, then decided to try her hand again at music. She moved to Nashville and worked as a waitress and a preschool teacher while she wrote songs and honed her talents.

Her first break came when Willie Nelson heard one of her demo tapes. He invited her to perform at his annual Farm Aid concert, a performance that led to a recording contract with Capitol Records. Before her debut album *Did I Shave My Legs for This?* was released, the record label underwent a change of leadership. That was the point at which Scott Hendricks was installed as head of the label.

Carter was terrified that the change would affect her album. She called her father in tears and he advised her not to jump to conclusions, that she would someday be a big star and would look back on the bad times and laugh.

As it turned out, Father did know best. Hendricks got behind the album in a big way and before his short tenure at Capitol was over, Deana Carter would prove to be the biggest star to emerge from the label under his watch.

New female stars were popping up all over Nashville. Canadian Terri Clark released her debut album in 1995 on Mercury Records, the same label that launched Shania Twain. Her first effort sold more than one million copies and established her as a real contender. That same year, a Texas group, Dixie Chicks, signed a recording contract with Sony Records. It took them three years to release their first album, *Wide Open Spaces*, but by early 1999 they were a dominant force on the charts.

Another new artist-in-waiting was Jo Dee Messina, a longtime friend of Tim McGraw's. She had moved to Nashville from Massachusetts, much as Tim had done from Louisiana, with nothing more substantial in her musical arsenal than an ill-defined dream. They became friends while working in the same dives and pledged that the first one to become a success would help the other.

Tim hit first, of course, and, true to his word, he helped Messina land a deal with his label, Curb Records. He invited her backstage for one of his Fan Fair appearances and introduced her to the label executives. What he didn't do was instruct her on how to behave. As a result, she broke one of the taboos of the music business and approached the executives with her own unique pitch.

"I was thinking," she said to the executives, "y'all need a redhead on this label." Socially it was equivalent to a commoner goosing a crown prince.

However, it turned out that they did need a redhead. Later, when Messina realized what she had done, she was shocked at her own boldness. "I didn't know that was not the right thing to do," she later explained to country.com. "If I had the rule book in front of me now, I don't think I would have come to where I am."

Another result of that backstage encounter was that Tim was anointed her producer. To everyone's surprise and delight, Messina's first album, *I'm Alright*, sold over two million copies, establishing her as the workingman's answer to Shania Twain, Faith Hill, and Deana Carter.

It is ironic that Faith was linked to two major stars of the 1990s, Jo Dee Messina and Deana Carter, through relationships with the men in her life, but it is not unusual considering the small circle of people involved with making country music. Even so, it shows a great deal of maturity and self-confidence on Faith's part that she could pursue her career while engaging in dinner-table conversations with the men in her life about the success of her competitors. How many male artists would be able to listen to the women in their lives praise talented men they worked with? Not many, that's for sure!

There is something special happening today among the women of country music. They are looking out not only for themselves, but for each other. That is because they believe they are part of a larger movement within music.

"Everything in life is cyclical, everything goes in cycles," said Deana Carter. "Women had a big musical surge in the early days; now here we go again. Women have great intuition and great foresight. It comes from that mothering gene. If you are a woman, you are going to try to mother something. To me, all the guys look alike and they sound alike. At least when Garth [Brooks] came out, he was different. We kind of cloned the men a little bit and the women have been allowed to flower."

As different as all the women are, there is a similarity in their mission. They want to be compared to male artists, but only in terms of sales and creative initiative. "I think that women are making some of the most unique music," said Terri Clark. "They all sound completely different from each other. Everyone has her own deal. Deana Carter has that Sheryl Crow–ish thing going. LeAnn Rimes sings her tail off and she has a retro thing. And Shania is doing a really different kind of country music. If you look at the females, it is really amazing. They're kicking everyone's butt."

Of course, along with the butt-kicking must go a modicum of diplomacy. Male power may be on the decline in the music industry, but it still must be reckoned with. Messina addressed that by partnering with McGraw. Shania did it by partnering with her husband, Mutt Lange. Terri Clark did it with a sense of self-parody. Known for her cowboy hat and boots, Clark fosters an aggressive image that makes a joke of such male-oriented signs of toughness. "It is a little amusing because I do have another side to me," she explained in 1997. "I have become known as the dirt-kicking, aggressive, in-your-face, take-no-BS-off-of-anybody [singer], but there is a softer side there."

By 2000, Clark discovered that being a female had its own power. She discarded the cowboy hat and replaced it with a giant python and a girlish hairdo. "I don't feel like I have to prove anything to anybody anymore," she told Wendy Newcomer of *Country Weekly*. "I don't have to get in everybody's face and prove how tough I am, how loud I can sing and how long I can hold a note."

Deana Carter approached it in a different way. "There have been times when people were condescending because I was a young woman— or maybe it was because of my youth," she says. "I have tried to live my life non-genderized. It keeps you one of the guys, but not threatening. It is really important to accept people for what they are"—the woman who made a million dollars by joking about shaving her legs pauses, chuckling softly to herself, then continues—"instead of what they have, physically or otherwise."

⟶ When Faith finally got down to the business of selecting songs for her next album, it had been almost three years since the release of *It Matters to Me*. She was in front of the public during that time, of course, performing in concert and making television appearances, but three years is an eternity to a recording artist. She knew the next album would have to be exceptional or she would have to look for a new line of work. That's just the way the system works.

"Three years is a long time between albums, but now, at age thirty, I'm married and have a little girl," Faith said through the Warner Bros. publicity department in 1998. "All of those changes have definitely given me inspiration I was needing and helped to influence this album."

The first thing Faith had to decide was what to do about a producer. The only producer she had ever had, Scott Hendricks, was obviously out of the question now. Tim suggested his producer, Byron Gallimore. She had worked with him on "It's Your Love" and it had been a good experience for her.

That was fine with Faith, but she decided to hedge her bets by employing a second producer, Dann Huff. He was one of the hottest guitarists in Nashville, but he also had proved himself to be a cutting-edge producer, someone who understood how to record crossover records that still maintained an identifiable country base. Additionally, he had a reputation for working well with women, a very important skill in Faith's eyes. He had worked with Lari White, and he was in the process of honing the studio sounds of the all-female group, SHeDAISY.

As always, finding the right songs offered the biggest challenge. Faith had changed, her entire personal life had been turned upside down, so she wanted her next album to reflect the new woman inside her and her happy marriage to Tim.

One of the worst things to arise from her divorce from Daniel and her breakup with Scott was the impact those failed relationships had had on her creativity and her self-confidence as a songwriter. The man who had encouraged her to write songs had ended up with a big chunk of her royalties, and the man who had so closely supervised her selection of songs had affected her self-confidence. The result of both those experiences was that she stopped trying to write songs. For the first time, she was going into a recording session with nothing of her own to offer.

The first song that Faith came across was "This Kiss," written by Robin Lerner, Annie Roboff, and Nashville recording artist Beth Nielsen Chapman. The three songwriters—a widow, a divorcée, and a single woman—wrote the song while vacationing at the beach, where they gathered in a circle and talked about the ups and downs of relationships, about how all it takes is one special person to make things right again. It is the way a woman is loved that matters, they concluded, not the reason why. Musically, the resulting song had pop momentum, an airy chorus, and a steel-guitar underpinning to keep it country.

Faith was crazy about the song from the moment she heard it. She could not get it out of her head and found herself singing it around the house, the way she had done as a child with Reba's and Tammy's songs. When the time came to record it, she invited Beth Nielsen Chapman into the studio and asked her to sing background. Chapman was stunned by the way Faith's interpretation transformed the song.

"Let Me Let Go," written by Steve Diamond and Dennis Morgan, is about not being able to let go of an old flame. Singing background is Vince Gill, who molded Faith's alto into a soprano with his unique voice. The song makes use of an acoustic guitar as its main engine, but accents it with a steel guitar and an entire string orchestra consisting of violins, cellos, and violas.

"You Give Me Love," written by the talented Matraca Berg, Jim Photoglo, and Harry Stinson, is about a woman who relies on her lover to save her from the bad times "when the world is cold." "Love Ain't Like That," written by Tim Gaetano and A. J. Masters, was composed as the result of the songwriters' frustration of trying to come up with a perfect last line for an up-tempo love song. "After rereading the lyrics one more time, I thought to myself, *Love ain't like that*," Gaetano explained to the Warner Bros. publicity department. "Right then I realized 'Love Ain't Like That' was the song we needed to write. After the first verse rolled out, it was easy to see it was something special. A. J. Masters and I got together and finished the song in one session. The theme of the song is simple: There is no formula for love . . . or the perfect love song."

"Better Days" was written by three friends sitting around talking about a mutual friend who was having a difficult time. For songwriters Bekka Bramlett, Billy Burnette, and Annie Roboff, it was a way to let the friend know that they cared. The song has a bluesy sound, as you would expect from Bramlett and Burnette, and features Bramlett singing background vocals.

"Just to Hear You Say that You Love Me" is a ballad that features Tim McGraw singing with Faith on the chorus and the later verses. Written by Diane Warren, it begins as a country song, then morphs into a power ballad of the Shania Twain variety.

Although "This Kiss" was the most commercial song to emerge from the session, two of the best cuts are "The Secret of Life" and "Somebody Stand by Me." The former, written by Gretchen Peters, is about a couple of guys, self-proclaimed losers, who are hanging out at the Starlight Bar, pondering the meaning of life. The way they figure, it all boils down to the fact that it is the little things that make life special. According to Peters, writing the song was a matter of wrapping music around a simple idea. "Don't listen to the TV gurus, don't buy the self-help books, don't waste your time searching for happiness," she told Warner Bros. "It's not a big Cecil B. DeMille moment anyway. It's usually waiting for you when you're not expecting it, in a cup of coffee, at a baseball game, or while you're driving and your favorite song comes on the radio. The secret of life is just recognizing it when it happens."

"Somebody Stand by Me," written by rocker Sheryl Crow and Todd Wolfe, is a blues/gospel ballad with a funky blues piano. The narrator asks, "Is God here tonight?"—a question that is followed by a plea to be grabbed up and set free. This is easily the most powerful song on the album, and it provides another fleeting glimpse of the *real* Faith Hill, the one whose blues/gospel heritage simply will not be denied, the one whose Little Elvis is given the nod to do his thing. No, you can't take the Mississippi out of the girl, but, then, why would you ever want to?

When the album was finished—many more songs were recorded than were actually used—Faith had five songs produced by Dann Huff and seven produced by Byron Gallimore. She felt it was the best thing she had ever done. For that reason, there was only one possible title for the album: *Faith*.

"Sometimes I joke and say I went through Egypt to get to Cheyenne, but I made it," Faith said in a Warner Bros. press release. "And really, there was no other way I could have made this album. It did take a long time, because I wanted to work with several different people. But in the end, the process was about discovering new places within myself."

Her feelings were not the only thing that had changed. Her voice had changed, grown deeper and fuller since her last album. She wondered if it was due to her throat surgery. Everyone said no, that it had nothing to due with the surgery, but she had no satisfactory explanation and it was beginning to bother her, chipping away at her self-confidence.

Finally, midway through making the record, Faith called Christian recording artist Amy Grant and confided in her. She told Grant she felt frustrated about the changes in her voice. "[Amy] said my hormones had gone ballistic, which, of course, they had," Faith told Michael Bane for *Country Music* magazine. "My vocal cords are fairly sensitive. Tim, though, is a horse—he can stay up for five days, do interviews and sing every night and nothing affects him. I'm not made that way."

Grant advised her to let up on herself and allow the hormones to run their course.

When *Faith* was released in spring 1998, country-music critics were friendly but not especially enthusiastic. The *New York Post* said the album was "listenable," but "not the greatest or worst country disk" ever recorded. Although that type of reception was not what Faith had hoped for, she knew that the most important critics were the ones who purchased the album and listened to the first single, "This Kiss," on the radio.

"My idea for the record was to focus a little more on the music that I do in my live shows," Faith said in a press release, "which is a lot livelier than anything I've ever put on record. And because I don't write [anymore], I really had to rely on songs that were out there. Miraculously, it all came together better than I had ever dreamed. It went into the refrigerator hot liquid and came out a beautiful salad, full of wonderful fruit."

Not only had Faith changed since her previous album, mainly because of her relationship with Tim, but the industry itself had undergone a traumatic reversal, thanks in part to the pioneering work of Shania Twain. The new country music had a pop sound to it because that was where the global audience that embraced Shania wanted it to go.

Gone were the days of "cheatin' hearts," because female CD-buyers wanted songs that dealt with self-empowerment and successful relationships. Gone was the twang, replaced by more sophisticated instrumentation and lyrics that could be understood by record-buyers in Germany and Japan, actually all over the world.

"I think *Faith* is a mirror reflection of where I am in my life," Faith said in a press release. "Musically for sure, there's no question about it. I could not have gone deeper to find what this record is. As far as the personal side, there are a lot of positive songs. And that's because I found it hard to sing about something sad and then go home to where I was exuding happiness all of the time. I felt I had to sing about things that were about the way I was really feeling."

One of the reasons Faith was so happy during the recording and release of the new album was because she and Tim had made another baby during the Thanksgiving holidays. The baby was due in August 1998. Of course, when word of her pregnancy filtered out into the Nashville music community, it made veterans dislike her even more.

Faith broke all the rules. She took time off to have one baby and now here she was pregnant again. She called herself a country singer, but she made records that appealed to pop audiences. The country-music establishment is almost exclusively male and it is hypersensitive to any changes in the music's format. Although no one ever came out and said it outright, Faith was public enemy number one among the old-timers.

Faith knew that, of course, knew that they talked about her behind her back, but she was at a point in her life where she really didn't care. What she cared most about were her family and her fans. Within weeks of the release of "This Kiss," it zoomed to the top of the country charts, proving that Faith's instincts about the song were correct. Soon half of America was singing the song around the house, just as Faith had done when she first heard it. Faith had made her fans happy, and that was more important than what the out-of-touch twang-tweakers on Music Row thought.

In March, even though she was four months pregnant, she joined Tim, George Strait, and John Michael Montgomery on a stadium tour that was scheduled to continue through June. Thus began a routine that Faith and Tim have maintained to this day: They took ten-month-old Gracie on the road with them. The way they see it, if they are going to live together as a family, they will have to learn to work together as a family. Their baby-sitting schedule is simple: one stays with Gracie while the other performs.

In April 1998, Tim and Faith came in off the road to participate in the Annual Academy of Country Music Awards show, telecast on CBS from Hollywood's Universal Amphitheater. Faith, dressed in angel white, was noticeably pregnant, while Tim, dressed in outlaw black, was noticeably proud to be in his beautiful wife's company.

Since the awards were presented to songs and albums from the previous year, Faith had no solo nominations. What she did have were four co-nominations with Tim for their hit single "It's Your Love."

Receiving awards that evening were Garth Brooks for Entertainer of the Year; George Strait for Top Male Vocalist and Album of the Year (for his critically acclaimed album, *Carrying Your Love with Me*); and Trisha Yearwood for Top Female Vocalist. It was a big evening for all the winners, but it was especially memorable to Tim and Faith, because their love ballad won in all four categories in which it was nominated—Song of the Year, Video of the Year, Single Record of the Year, and Vocal Event of the Year.

That's a lot of trophies to take home—Tim and Faith each received four—as was acknowledged by Faith who jokingly told reporters she would have to buy a new piece of furniture to house the eight awards. More seriously, she told a reporter for country.com that the song was "just logical for the two of us, as a couple." Tim added that he thought people could relate to the song. "I think that probably everybody has been in that same type situation in one way or another."

When someone asked where Gracie was, they said that she was safely tucked away in a nearby hotel. "Having a child puts everything into perspective, I believe, into the right places," Faith told the Cable News Network. "[Gracie] just brings such joy to our lives. You can't really describe it. It's just awesome."

It was shaping up to be a phenomenal summer for the couple. By May, *Faith* would be number 2 on the country charts and by June it would be in the Top Ten on the pop charts. Concert audiences were wildly enthusiastic to see the couple, but they were especially happy to see Faith, who was beginning to eclipse her husband in popularity, a result of the crossover success of "This Kiss."

Tim and Faith circled back to Nashville in June to participate in Fan Fair 1998, along with LeAnn Rimes, Deana Carter, Terri Clark, Vince Gill, Jo Dee Messina, Bryan White, and others. After a brief respite, they went back out on the road again, with Tim going east and Faith and Gracie going west.

In July, Faith did a performance at the Adams County FairFest in Hastings, Nebraska. For weeks there had been rumors that she would be a no-show because of reports of exhaustion—she was, after all, eight months pregnant—but she thrilled the crowd of four thousand by taking the stage at the appointed hour.

Faith performed some of her biggest hits, including "The Hard Way," "Take Me as I Am," "It Matters to Me," and the song that sent everyone into wild applause, "This Kiss." Maybe the studio bigwigs on Music Row did not understand the song, but it was clearly appreciated by her fans in the heartland.

"Thanks for being so sweet to welcome an eight-and-a-half . . . ooh . . . almost nine-months' pregnant woman," Faith told the audience, according to Holley Hatt of the *Hastings Tribune*. During band introductions, Faith brought Gracie onstage so that the audience could see her. Each time Faith introduced one of the band members, Gracie clapped along with the audience. Before the introductions were over, reported Hatt, it was difficult to tell who the audience was clapping harder for—Gracie or the band.

One of the first questions Faith asked when the tour bus rolled onto the fairgrounds was if there were any craft stores in town. Told that the only thing close to that was a Ben Franklin store in downtown Hastings,

Faith said that sounded good to her. What she needed were some craft projects to occupy her on the bus ride to Wyoming.

From the stage, Faith chatted with the audience, depending on her folksy, Mississippi background to help her make new friends in a community that was larger than her hometown of Star, but not by much. "My daughter had a blast," she told the audience, describing her shopping experience in Hastings. "We walked in the front door and she spotted this little shopping cart just her size. She shopped until she dropped."

Once the concert ended, fans lined the fence to wave good-bye.

Two weeks later, Faith was in the Baptist Hospital in Nashville to give birth to her second daughter, Maggie Elizabeth, who was born at 9:48 A.M. on August 12, 1998. She weighed in at six pounds nine ounces and stretched out to an impressive nineteen inches.

Two years earlier, Faith had wondered if she would ever have the things she wanted in life. Now she had *everything*—a husband she loves, two children, and a career that was soaring to heights not seen since Shania Twain's initial success.

Only weeks after giving birth to Maggie, Faith was out in public again, starting with Tim's annual Swampstock event in Louisiana, where Faith's "team" consisted of Chely Wright, Sons of the Desert, Jo-el Sonnier, and the Clark Family Experience, then on to the Country Music Association Awards show. It was the first time many in the Nashville music community had seen Faith since her marriage to Tim.

Faith looked radiant that night, dressed in an elegant low-cut black dress and sporting a new shortened hairdo that she chose before going out on her 1998 concert tour. Faith was nominated in four categories: Female Vocalist of the Year (against Patty Loveless, Martina McBride, Lee Ann Womack, and Trisha Yearwood); Single of the Year; Music Video of the Year; and Vocal Event of the Year (a duet with Tim, "Just to Hear You Say that You Love Me").

Tim also received four nominations: Entertainer of the Year (against Garth Brooks, Vince Gill, George Strait, and Brooks and Dunn); Male Vocalist of the Year (against Garth Brooks, Vince Gill, Collin Raye, and

George Strait); Album of the Year (against Brooks's *Sevens*, Strait's *One Step at a Time*, and Loveless's *Long Stretch of Lonesome*); and Vocal Event of the Year (with Faith).

When Tim was announced the winner in the prestigious Album of the Year category, Faith hugged him tightly, her face clearly reflecting the emotion she felt. Tim took the stage with his producers, Byron Gallimore and James Stroud. "I've got the best guys in the world," he said, looking admiringly at the two men. "Not only are they great producers, they are great people."

Unfortunately, Faith took home only one award that evening—Music Video of the Year. It was a slap in the face from the CMA and everyone knew why. The conservative wing of country music, the one that considers twang a measuring rod of artistic honesty, felt that Faith's music had too much pop content. Their favorite line was: "She can't sing, but she sure looks pretty!" The only award they could stomach giving her was one that recognized her looks over her music. Faith took her defeats with good grace, but the tears must have flowed like rain when she got home.

One month later, she showed up at the CMA's fortieth-anniversary television special that was taped at the Nashville arena. She performed that evening, doing "It's Your Love" with Tim, a performance that delighted the audience.

One of the things that she liked best about the evening, she told the Nashville *Tennessean*, was that she didn't have to worry about winning any awards (none were presented): "You don't have to sit there with your hands sweating, clutching something to where your knuckles are so white. It's a lot less pressure."

By November, Faith was out on the road performing, promoting her latest single, "Let Me Let Go." That same month, she appeared on Jay Leno's *Tonight Show* and the following month she did *The Rosie O'Donnell Show*, where she performed "Let Me Let Go" with a five-piece band.

It was a performance that offered a cornucopia of opposing images. There was Faith the supremely confident artist struggling with her microphone stand, often clutching it with both hands as she looked ill at ease. There was Faith the happily married woman pleading, lyrically at least, for her lover to please let her let go out of the relationship. And there was Faith the star, dressed to kill in a navy sweater and matching slacks, sitting down at the desk with O'Donnell, oozing love for her two children.

O'Donnell, herself a mother of two children, wasted no time getting to the heart of what everyone in the audience was thinking: "You look amazingly fit for having had a baby four months ago."

Faith responded that her good figure was due to Gracie, her nineteen-month-old "trainer" who kept her going at full throttle. "It's really cool to watch Maggie watch Gracie play," she added. "Maggie doesn't really do anything but poop and sleep and eat. She's starting to raise her head and play a little bit, but it's fun to look into her eyes and watch Gracie play."

Faith said she really enjoyed having the children travel with her on the tour bus, but it made her wonder how they would react if they attended some of the wilder venues she has played in her career, such as the Mississippi tobacco-spitting contest.

O'Donnell expressed disbelief that Faith would ever play such an uncouth event. Faith told her all about it, ending with, "I'm so glad I don't do that anymore."

Like two mothers sitting on a park bench, the guest and the host talked about their children throughout the entire interview. O'Donnell asked Faith if Gracie had ever mimicked her by saying a "bad word." Oh yes, Faith responded, adding that Gracie was playing at the table one day when they heard her use the "it" word. "What was so impressive about it was that she knew when to use it," Faith marveled.

Tim and Faith ended 1998 focused on their children. After bribing Gracie with a few cookies, they persuaded her to design a wreath for their Christmas card, a task she undertook with brushes, sponges, and as much green and red paint as she could splash within the confines of a Christmas card. The finished card carried the credit, "Art for cookies, illustrated by Gracie McGraw."

Faith and Tim began 1999 with a New Year's Eve celebration at the Gaylord Entertainment Center in Nashville. Less than one week after the New Year's Eve bash, Faith and Tim learned that they both were nominated for Grammys at the upcoming show at the Shrine Auditorium in Los Angeles.

Faith received nominations in the categories of Female Country Artist of the Year; Country Song of the Year ("This Kiss"); and Country Album of the Year (*Faith*). The couple received a joint nomination in the "Country Collaboration" category for their duet, "Just to Hear You Say that You Love Me." It was the only nomination received by Tim.

Neither performed at the show, hosted by Rosie O'Donnell, but they were treated to a blistering lineup of performances, including sets by Madonna, Ricky Martin, Sheryl Crow, Luciano Pavarotti, Vince Gill, and Aerosmith. The CMA and ACM awards are more important to country artists, from a career standpoint, but Grammys are usually the most satisfying, for they are granted by voters who mostly work in other areas of music such as rock, pop, and rhythm and blues.

Unfortunately, it was not in the cards for either Faith or Tim to receive pats on the back that night. Winning the Country Album of the Year award was the Dixie Chicks, for their hit *Wide Open Spaces*. The Female Country Artist of the Year award and the Country Song award went to Shania for "You're Still the One." Edging Faith and Tim out in the Country Collaboration were Clint Black and twelve other artists for "Same Old Train."

It was a disappointing way to begin the new year, but *Faith* was still in the Top Ten on the country charts and still strong on the Top 50 charts. Besides, Faith had plenty of other projects to focus on upon her return to Nashville, the most important of which was the completion of her new album, *Breathe*.

As she did on her previous album, she worked with the same two producers, Byron Gallimore and Dann Huff, although this time around Huff got only four cuts on an album of thirteen songs. Faith told interviewers during the promotion of her previous album that she looked for songs that reflected how she felt about life at the time she recorded the album. She said her albums should be viewed as an extension of her life.

"The music that I make has to be right for me at the right time," Faith told Warner Bros. "It has to have meaning. When I sing a song, I am in that song . . . and hopefully people hear and feel that. I can't draw that line of trust with my fans if I don't sing from my heart every time I'm in front of a microphone."

If so, it raises interesting questions about her state of mind while recording *Breathe*. "Breathe," the power ballad written by Holly Lamar and Stephanie Bentley, may be construed as offering more insight into her passionate love for Tim, but other songs such as "If My Heart Had Wings," written by Annie Roboff and J. Fred Knobloch, are about trying to stay together despite the physical distances that sometimes separate couples. Then there is Bruce Springsteen's "If I Should Fall Behind," a song about the unpredictability of love. "It was the first time I ever cried while in the studio," she told her record label. "I couldn't have made this album and not recorded [it]. After seeing and meeting Bruce at one of his shows, that song took on a special meaning for me. The lyrical content is devastating and the message just hits you in your soul."

Other songs on the new album include "What's In It for Me," written my Billy Burnette, Bekka Bramlett, and Annie Roboff (who contributed to three songs on the album). It is a bluesy, Bonnie Raitt–type number about not giving it away for free. "The Way You Love Me," written by Keith Follese and Michael Delaney, offers 1980s-style instrumentation with a modern melody that draws its energy from a string of delicious overlapping background vocals.

"Let's Make Love," written by Chris Lindsey, Marv Green, Bill Luther, and Aimee Mayo, is one of the few songs on the album that maintains a traditional country feel, although its smooth, silky sound is upstaged by lyrics about making love all night. Sung with Tim as a romantic duet, it sounds remarkably similar to their previous duet.

"You Bring Out the Elvis," written by Leif Larsson and Louise Hoffsten, may not be the best song on the album, but it is one of the most entertaining. In a funky, blues-rock beat, it tells the story of a woman who has been a slave to the beat for too long. Now she wants to swing her hips and burst out into song. Faith must have grinned the entire time she recorded this song. Certainly the Little Elvis inside her enjoyed the joke.

While working on the album, she realized that she was going to have problems with the country-music establishment. The songs sounded much too contemporary to be country music. She knew she would be blasted for recording an album that ignored tradition, but if that was the type of music she was feeling, why shouldn't she record it?

"I reached a place last year, a certain level of success, and now it's time to go to another place," she explained to her record label. "In order to succeed you can't be afraid to fail. I consider [this album] a mixture of musical styles that reflects my love for country, pop, gospel, and rhythm and blues. Yes, I decided to take some chances here musically—as an artist that is who I am. I've always tried to achieve and to do better."

Faith took a major step that spring in promoting her crossover appeal by appearing on the *VH1 Divas Live '99* broadcast on April 13 from New York's Beacon Theater. Starring Tina Turner, Whitney Houston, Elton John, Brandy, and LeAnn Rimes, it provided Faith with national exposure in a noncountry format.

Just being on the same stage with Tina Turner, who performed "Proud Mary" and "Simply the Best," was a thrill Faith talked about for months. In addition to performing a duet with pop and R&B star Brandy ("Everything I Do I Do for You"), Faith sang her biggest hit to date in 1999, "This Kiss."

Actually, Faith was invited to the event because of Brandy. A couple of weeks earlier, Faith had done a Cover Girl cosmetics photo shoot with Brandy and supermodel Niki Taylor. When VH1 production executives informed Brandy she could invite a guest performer, she chose fellow Mississippian Faith Hill.

The Cover Girl deal seemingly came from nowhere. One day Faith received a telephone call from the cosmetics company offering her a lucrative deal to be a spokesperson and the next day she was in New York to sign the contract and begin a photo shoot with Brandy and Niki Taylor.

"I'm extremely excited to be a part of the Cover Girl family," Faith said in a press release. "Cover Girl conveys a positive message, which reminds us that being beautiful on the inside is just as important as being beautiful on the outside."

Nineteen ninety-nine was turning out to be a big year for Tim McGraw. His new album *A Place in the Sun* sold over 250,000 units its first week of release. Its first single, "Please Remember Me," made the top five in only a matter of weeks. There was nothing really unexpected in the album, except perhaps a harmony duet with country artist Patty Loveless. Tim had wanted to sing with her for years, but not until recently had their schedules allowed it. The song was "Jewel of the South," about how to make something positive out of leaving a relationship.

"The older you get, the more you have to sing about," Tim told Wendy Newcomer of *Country Weekly*. "I feel like I'm starting to get a handle on this business. . . . Just like anybody, you mature and grow with what you're doing."

There was trouble on the horizon with his record label, Curb Records, but for now he didn't see how life could possibly get any better. One of the unexpected things he had to learn to deal with was his wife's growing popularity. At times, he sometimes seemed just as taken by Faith's changing image as were her fans.

"This has been the best time of my life," Tim told country.com. "It's been a time for me to really evaluate where I'm going and what I'm doing—to focus my direction. When you have a family, that changes your whole perspective on what you do and what you want to get out of what you do."

Tim was not at a place, emotionally, where he was able to feed off of his relationship with Faith in a way that affected his music, but Faith certainly was. She used every strong emotion, every nuance, she found in her relationships with Tim and the children to enhance the creativity of her music.

In many ways, the standards for women in country music were higher than for the men, and the margin for error was smaller. If a woman did not put everything she had into it, the odds were good that someone else would pick up the mantle.

By March 1999, Faith Hill, Shania Twain, and the Dixie Chicks were the undisputed leaders. The Chicks' album *Wide Open Spaces* had sold four million units, Twain's 1997 release *Come On Over* was at an astonishing eight million, and Faith's self-titled album was at more than two million and still registering in the Top Ten. But there were other women in the wings, strong contenders such as the energetic sister trio SHe-DAISY, Australian-born Jamie O'Neal, Lee Ann Womack, Sara Evans, and Tim McGraw protégée Jo Dee Messina.

"I think it's really sad, but we have tried to clone our male artists for some reason," RCA Records A&R executive Renee Bell told this author. "Seventy percent of the guys signed in this town all sound alike—and they're not selling records. The female artists are so different. I don't think there are many, if any, female artists who sound alike, and their songs are so different."

Bell is amused that so many of the songs recorded by women are written by men. "I think women are so different," she says. "I still don't know how [men and women] ever get together. I think women are very complicated creatures. I think married men with daughters could probably get it better than a single guy could. I'm sure that most of the songs written by men are by happily married men who have been in long relationships."

⟶ By 1999, Faith's physical beauty was an issue in her career, so much so that strategic planners in her organization were more concerned about her hair than about her music. Her hair had changed drastically during the course of her career. It went from dark-blonde for the first album, to a reddish blonde tint, then on to a tight-curl natural blonde look and, most recently, the platinum-blonde look she maintained throughout her Spontaneous Combustion tour with Tim in 2000. It was the latter look she enjoyed most, primarily because of the big ringlet curls that gave her an exotic look she thought was appropriate for a crossover country singer.

There were some problems with that hairstyle, however. One night she put her hair up in heated rollers, unaware of what could happen when the chemicals in the curling product reacted with the heat from the curlers. When she removed the curlers from her hair, she had a new style, all right—it was bright pink!

Faith's look for the *Faith* tour was the most radical in many ways, for it gave her a close-cropped look reminiscent of Marilyn Monroe. She called it her "messy" look, primarily because all she did after showering was dry it off and give her head a good shake before beginning her day.

Judging by the continued success of her last album, *Faith*—it remained in the Top Ten—she could have gone out on tour bald and been a smashing success. It was her first time headlining a tour and she displayed a new side of herself by taking charge with impressive authority.

The downside of being an opening act, as she had discovered on her previous tour, is the necessity of using the headliner's equipment and stage presentation. She was emphatic with tour planners that she must have every detail of her stage presentation done exactly the way she wanted it. If she wanted to rent a grand piano for use on the stage, then, by golly, she would rent a grand piano (she did).

The biggest mistake anyone could ever make about Faith is to assume that she is as soft and appealing on the inside as she is on the outside. That's not the girl that Ted and Edna Perry raised and unleashed on the world. The Country Music Association found that out later in the summer, when its television committee turned down her request to sing her lead-off single from her new album, *Breathe*.

The CMA insisted that she sing her most recent single, "The Secret of Life." Faith didn't want to sing an old song. She wanted to do a new song. Why couldn't she sing the song of her choice? Rules are rules, the committee told her—take it or leave it.

There was more to it than that, of course (there always is). The Country Music Association did not much care for Faith Hill's glamorous appearance, her pop-oriented music or her Los Angeles manager Gary Borman. That was obvious in the fact that, despite her enormous success, the CMA had given only two awards to her—Vocal Event of the Year, for her duet with Tim on his song, "It's Your Love," and Video of the Year for "This Kiss." Neither of those awards paid tribute to Faith as a recording artist.

When news of the impasse reached the media, the CMA was asked why it would not allow Faith to perform her new song. The organization responded that only previous Entertainers of the Year or current Entertainer of the Year nominees were allowed to perform new material.

Passions on the issue ran so high that Curb Records president Mike Curb resigned from the television committee. He pointed out that seven of the sixteen members on the committee worked for record labels and he suggested that everyone resign to avoid the appearance of a conflict of interest. Interestingly, Faith's record label, Warner Bros., had no representation on the committee.

"There is politics," CMA executive director Ed Benson told *Tennessean* writer Tom Roland. "Anybody who tells you there shouldn't be politics in this process just fell off the turnip truck. It's my responsibility to make sure politics does not override the interest of creating the best television show for the industry."

For a time it appeared Faith would be a no-show at the awards show, which was scheduled to be broadcast live by CBS Television; but at the last minute the television network stepped in and told the CMA committee to allow Faith to sing the song of her choice. "If Faith isn't in the show, everybody loses," explained a spokeswoman for CBS.

Despite the public bloodletting prior to the show, the Thirty-third Annual CMA Awards aired without incident, with Faith Hill singing the song of her choice, "Breathe." In many ways, it was one of the most interesting evenings in the show's history.

In addition to the dispute over what song Faith could sing, there was a confrontation with country-music legend George Jones over the television committee's instructions that he sing an abbreviated version of his nominated song, "Choices." Rather than edit his song, Jones declined to participate in the awards show. Alan Jackson thought Jones had been mistreated and paid tribute to him by adding a chorus and a verse from Jones's song to his own nominated single, "Pop a Top."

Faith was nominated in several categories and the question on everyone's mind that evening was whether the CMA would allow either of the McGraws to win an award. As it turned out, Tim was given awards for Album of the Year and Male Vocalist of the Year, but Faith was given no awards. Her hit single, "This Kiss," was named Song of the Year, but the honors went to the songwriters and not to Faith. That did not really surprise her. Since Faith's career began, the CMA had chosen Pam Tillis, Alison Krauss, Patty Loveless, Trisha Yearwood, and Martina McBride as its Female Vocalists of the Year, while ignoring the contributions of two of country music's biggest performers, Shania Twain and Faith Hill.

What those two women were doing with country music was the subject of intense debate among males within the industry. Some of those feelings erupted at the awards show, most notably from longtime Faith Hill friend Vince Gill, who was obviously torn over his friendship with Faith and his belief that perhaps she was going too far with her music. During the acceptance speech for his award for "My Kind of Woman, My Kind of Man," a duet he recorded with Patty Loveless, he cautioned new artists not to lose sight of country music's conservative tradition. Said Gill: "Don't lose sight of our roots. They're very important to us."

Of course, the most blatant political statement made that evening came from Tim McGraw—and he made it without saying a word. During the performance of his nominated song, "My Best Friend," huge images of Faith appeared on the screen behind him. Everyone got the message loud and clear.

Faith left the theater that evening bloodied but not bowed.

Not long after finishing *Breathe*, Faith went to work on the video. Like the album, it would be groundbreaking in the way it unabashedly depicted Faith's sensuality in a number of scenes in which the singer was filmed beneath the satin sheets of a bed. It is arguably the most sensual video by a country-music artist to date.

After the video was completed, the director, Lili Fini Zanuck, told reporters that the process had made Faith noticeably uncomfortable. "She just doesn't believe that she's as beautiful as she is," Zanuck told *US Weekly*. "She'll be sexy for the camera, but as soon as you say 'Cut,' she's not comfortable."

Interestingly, Zanuck, following the dictum long observed by fashion photographers, that sensuality is best transformed to film through the creative use of arms and legs, not bare flesh, brought out Faith's inherent sensuality with a focus on her graceful arms and legs and by allowing her to simply be herself. It is a remarkable video on several levels.

What Zanuck wanted to create in the video was movielike in its approach to sensuality, explained the co-producer of the Oscar-winning feature film *Driving Miss Daisy*. "I wanted to do something you used to see in movies all the time, which is putting a woman on a pedestal," Zanuck told *Entertainment Weekly*.

Faith was happy with the video, but felt compelled to call her mother to warn her about its slightly erotic content. Edna's response was typical of their new adult relationship: She told Faith she was too old to be asking for approval from her mother and Faith responded that she was not too old to care what her mother thought.

When *Breathe* was released in November 1999, the album debuted at number one on the country charts, the single "Breathe" debuted at number one on the pop charts, and the video went into heavy rotation on Country Music Television and VH1, establishing Faith as the most exciting artist of the new millennium. Despite snubs from the CMA, Faith was poised to experience the wildest ride of her life.

What's in It for Me

Faith and Tim began 2000 with a New Year's Eve celebration at the Gaylord Entertainment Center in Nashville. For the past three years, Tim had hosted the event, making it—with nearly twenty thousand people in attendance—the city's biggest party of the year. He had never thought of himself as a party animal, but there he was hosting one that people would talk about for weeks.

In addition to Faith, other performers included the Clark Family Experience and newcomer Jessica Andrews, the teenager who had toured with Faith during the previous summer. Andrews received a cheer from the audience when she announced that she was wearing pants Faith had loaned to her for the concert. They were the same tight, black leather pants Faith wore in her "Let's Go to Vegas" video. The teen had approached Faith several days before the concert, complaining that she had nothing to wear. Faith generously opened her closet and told her to take whatever she needed. Choosing was not a problem for Andrews: those tight black pants were . . . oh, so sexy!

Faith performed a number of her hits during her hourlong set, including "Breathe," "The Secret of Life," and her duet with Tim, "It's Your Love," but it was the final song of the evening that attracted the most attention. Minutes before midnight, Faith sang "This Kiss," and then shared a public kiss with Tim as the New Year—and the new millennium—was celebrated by the cheering audience and viewers of ABC Television nationwide.

Four weeks later Faith performed before an even larger audience. As a loyal supporter of the Tennessee Titans, Faith agreed to sing the National Anthem at Super Bowl XXXIV, which matched the Titans against the St. Louis Rams. The contest was held at the Georgia Dome in Atlanta before an estimated stadium/television audience of over one billion people.

In the beginning, the Tennessee Titans were a team only a country-music songwriter could appreciate. It would not be until 1999 that the team would have a stadium in Nashville, which meant that the Titans played their "home" games in various, far-from-world-class stadiums around the state. The first year the team played in its new Nashville stadium it had an 8–0 record at home. It was good enough to catapult the team through the playoffs and into the Super Bowl.

It is easy to see why the tenderhearted Faith would embrace the luckless Titans. No team in America needed true-blue friends quite so much. Besides that, Nashville's honor was at stake and, by association, the honor of country music.

Faith and Tim attended every one of the Titan's playoff games, cheering the team on to victory. After the Titans racked up a victory in the first playoff game, Tim wore the same clothes to each of the other games to bring the team good luck. Faith did not take her support that far, but to the delight of those sitting around her, she jumped and screamed like the Star cheerleader she used to be.

Two days before the Super Bowl, Faith astonished reporters at a press conference by pumping her fists in the air and shouting, "Go Titans!" Isn't the singer of the National Anthem supposed to be neutral? Heck no, Faith asserted. She promised not to wear a Titans jersey when she sang, but she could not promise to keep her team spirit hidden from public view.

"This is a career highlight for me," she told Tasneem Ansariyah-Grace of the Nashville *Tennessean*. "I have had the opportunity to sing the National Anthem for a couple of playoff games, but I never thought about making it to the 'big' game."

Faith will always be a cheerleader for the home team, no matter what the team is called, and that is one of the reasons why her fans are so devoted to her. When the time came for Faith to step up to the microphone, she performed with perfection, singing not only with conviction, but with more than a little Mississippi soul. The Titans themselves leaped into the air when she finished, grinning ear-to-ear as if they—and they alone—had the secret weapon for victory. They had Faith.

Unfortunately the Titans lost to the Rams in the final seconds of the game, giving rival St. Louis bragging rights to the 23–16 victory. Faith was crestfallen, but she took solace in the fact that she had given the team her very best cheer.

Early in January 2000, Faith's hopes for a Grammy were raised when it was announced that she had been nominated for an award in the Female Country Vocal Performance category for her song "Let Me Let Go." Tim was nominated in the Male Country Vocal Performance category. Unfortunately, when the winners were announced in late February at Los Angeles' Staples Center, neither Faith nor Tim took home awards. The big country winners were Shania Twain, Dixie Chicks, and Vince Gill.

Faith left Los Angeles disappointed once again, but she would soon be asked to return to the city on an unprecedented mission of mercy. For the moment, all her efforts were focused on *Breathe*. From mid-January through mid-April, the album hung in the Top Twenty of the pop album charts, an early indication that sales would be impressive. She may not have been on target with stuffed-shirt Grammy voters—after all, they had ignored Elvis, giving him recognition only for his gospel recordings—but she had a natural instinct for recording music the public appreciated.

The only thing Faith could really count on at this point in her career was surprises. Her life was filled with them. When Cover Girl had called in 1999 and asked her to become a spokeswoman for their products, no one was more surprised than Faith. She had never thought of herself as supermodel material.

Not agreeing with that was Pepsi, which signed her to do a series of television advertisements created by BBDL of New York. The ads paired Faith with eight-year-old Hallie Eisenberg, the New Jersey grammar-school student who received the nickname "the Pepsi Girl" after appearing in a series of high-profile television ads with Marlon Brando, Aretha Franklin, and Joe Pesci. In each ad, the fifty-one-pound scene-stealer pantomimed the voices of the stars, becoming, in effect, a free spirit possessed of mysterious ventriloquist-like powers.

For the commercial with Faith, the ad agency scripted a scene in which Hallie taught the singer the proper phrasing for its *"dah-da-dah-dah-da"* jingle. There was only one shoot for the project, but the ad agency was able to weave two separate commercials from the footage it obtained. One showed Faith onstage successfully singing the jingle, with Hallie seated at a piano giving an approving nod. It was a very effective piece of work that played off of Faith's beauty and celebrity as a singer, and Hallie's precocious, dimple-studded perkiness, a quality that *Newsweek* once described as "beyond cute."

Suddenly Faith's manager Gary Borman found himself fielding so many endorsement offers that he could barely keep up with them all. Her income from sources outside music was quickly overtaking what she earned as a performer. Of all the unexpected telephone calls Borman received during this time, none was more compelling than the one he received at one o'clock in the morning from Lili Zanuck, who, as producer of the 2000 Academy Awards, had a special request.

"Where's Faith?" asked Zanuck, who had directed the "Breathe" video.

Gorman responded that she had just come in off the road and was at home, surely sound asleep at that hour (three o'clock Nashville time). Zanuck told him that she had an emergency and urgently needed Faith's help. Her emergency was spelled W-h-i-t-n-e-y.

Just two days before the Grammys were scheduled to be telecast, problems with Whitney Houston had developed during rehearsals. The pop diva had accepted an invitation to participate in a special tribute medley with Garth Brooks, Queen Latifah, Isaac Hayes, and Ray Charles. Everything seemed to be going as planned until Houston had a disagreement with musical director Burt Bacharach during a rehearsal.

The thirty-nine-year-old singer walked around in circles, humming tunes (not the ones being practiced) and playing an "invisible" keyboard, according to *Newsweek*. " 'As soon as you saw her, you knew she was out of it. . . . It was quite sad,' " reported the magazine, quoting an unidentified source.

The following day, when Houston showed up for the final rehearsal, her behavior was such that Bacharach asked her to leave the show. Early the next morning, at one o'clock, Zanuck called Borman and pleaded for his help. It was less than forty-eight hours until showtime.

Borman called Faith early that morning and told her that she had been asked to replace Houston. That meant catching the next flight out of Nashville to Los Angeles. Without hesitation, Faith said she would do it. It all happened so fast there was no time for nervousness. Said Borman to VH1. "She shines in those situations. She really does."

Later that day, as Faith tossed her clothes into a suitcase and then made a mad dash to the airport, the Academy of Motion Picture Arts and Sciences told the media that Houston had withdrawn from the show because of a sore throat, a story that was backed up by Houston's publicist. *Newsweek* stuck to its story, reporting "increasingly odd behavior" by the singer. It probably would not have been much of a story if Houston had not been involved in a marijuana controversy earlier in the year at a Hawaiian airport.

Faith stayed above the fray, performing "The Way We Were" and "Somewhere Over the Rainbow" before a worldwide television audience. She looked cool and collected, and viewers had no idea of the turmoil that had occurred behind the scenes.

After the show, there were reports that Garth Brooks was peeved because of Faith's surprise appearance. The substitution did not meet with the approval of Brooks—who was supposed to be the only country act in the medley—and the *New York Post* reported that he was "literally in tears." A spokeswoman at Capitol Records defended Brooks, saying that his emotions were the result of concern he felt for Houston, whom he had known for a long time.

All that said, nothing mattered so much as the fact that Faith had bailed out the Oscars and delivered one of the most memorable performances of the evening. For those who know Faith, it was simply another confirmation that she could walk through a field of dung and emerge smelling like a sweet magnolia.

Another unexpected call Borman received was from VH1. After the success of its *Divas 1999* show, the cable network decided to produce a similar show, to be titled *VH1 Divas 2000: A Tribute to Diana Ross*. Producers wanted to book Faith for the show. Appearing with her would be Mariah Carey, Donna Summer, and the top diva herself, Diana Ross. Of course, there was no way Faith would say no to that.

The show was taped at Madison Square Garden in what was later described as a "grueling" five-hour session. Already scheduled to do a major feature on Faith, *US* magazine sent writer Josh Rottenberg along for the ride. Backstage with Faith, he observed Tim McGraw bring a slice of pepperoni pizza into his wife's dressing room. "Eat," he said sternly, afraid she had not had enough to eat that day.

Faith ignored the pizza, choosing instead to talk about her feelings. "I'm not nervous," she explained. "I just don't know who it's going to be yet. . . . I don't know any of them . . . they probably all know each other already."

Faith was not concerned about her abilities, about the way she would sound standing next to the other pop divas, but she was fearful of being excluded from "the group." And who could blame her?

Donna Summer's ability to bond with the other women was pretty much an unknown, but Mariah was known to be shy and clannish, and Diana Ross had a reputation as a world-class bitch. Faith wondered how they would react to her. Besides their personalities, there was the fact that she was the only non-ethnic diva on the stage. Would they hate her because she was white? Would they hate her because she was from Mississippi? Would they make snide comments because she is a country singer?

As it turned out, Faith had nothing to worry about. Everyone was friendly enough toward Faith, though it was apparent onstage that Mariah and Donna felt more connected to Diana than to Faith, and perhaps that was to be expected. The only diva who appeared uncomfortable before the cameras was Diana, who seemed suspicious of Mariah's eagerness to be performing on the stage next to her.

With her perpetually windswept blonde hair airborne, as if she were being towed by a speedboat, Faith was easily the most glamorous woman on the stage that night, although Mariah and Diana did raise the temperature with a battling, bare-thighs performance of "Stop in the Name of Love." Oddly, Diana insisted on wearing Mariah's gold dress, a decision that was counterpointed by Mariah's decision not to wear pantyhose (or anything else) beneath the dress given to her.

Nothing really explosive happened during the taping—unlike the taping for the previous divas special, when Tina Turner had criticized Elton John's piano-playing, sending him rushing offstage in a huff—but the accumulation of small problems did take its toll on the production staff.

"There were moments," VH1 executive vice president Wayne Isaak told *Entertainment Weekly*, "where we had to take some really deep breaths." Among the problems he listed: hair and clothing issues, a microphone that did not meet Diana's expectation, and a band the headliner had only worked with once.

By the time the taping was over, Faith was happy and relieved to escape without incident. Nothing bad happened. It was just that looming potential for trouble that sapped all her energy. The next day, she and Tim boarded a jet and flew to Paris, where they shot the video for their duet, "Let's Make Love."

The video is a testament to the couple's love for each other. Shot in black-and-white, it depicts the couple as they were at that moment— lovers in Paris. "[We] weren't groping each other," she told CDNOW.com. "We spared people in the studio [but] it was a special moment for us. It was nice just being in there together, doing it—the song."

Faith makes no pretenses about a higher meaning for the song. "[It] is pretty direct," she told *Redbook*. "It just flat out says, 'Let's make love, get over here, take your clothes off, and let's get right to it.'"

After they recorded the song, she later confided, they rushed home to do for real what they had only sung about in the studio, only they ran into a roadblock of sorts—daughters Gracie and Maggie wanted their undivided attention.

⟶ The Academy of Country Music had always been kind to Faith Hill. Between 1993 and 1999, it awarded eleven awards to the singer. That compares to three awards during that time from the Country Music Association. One reason for that is the ACM's more progressive attitudes toward country music. "Sexy" does not offend the ACM; on the contrary, sex appeal is viewed as a natural accompaniment of music.

In May 2000, Faith and Tim traveled to Los Angeles to participate in the ACM awards show at the Universal Amphitheater. It wasn't Faith's biggest year ever with the ACM, but she did take home two awards: Top Country Video for "Breathe," and Top Female Vocalist.

Accepting the video award with Faith was director Lili Zanuck. "This is really not my award," Faith told the audience. "This is Lili's award. She is an amazing director. I am honored to know [her]." Looking as if she might be experiencing her first bout of stage fright, Zanuck reluctantly stepped up to the microphone and thanked Faith.

Backstage, ACM producer Dick Clark grouped Faith and the Dixie Chicks together for a live interview. Looking directly at Faith, he asked, "Would you ever dye your hair?"

"Would I or have I?" responded Faith.

"Would you ever dye it brown?"

Eyeing Emily Robison, the blonde-turned-brunette Dixie Chick, she tactfully answered, "Absolutely."

Without missing a beat, Emily chimed in, "You get more respect."

Of course, in Emily's case, her switch from blonde to brunette was merely a return to her natural hair color.

Faith and Tim performed their new duet, "Let's Make Love," with the Paris-made video playing in the background, but they were nominated for no awards in the duet category. When Faith took the stage, amid a standing ovation, to accept her Top Female Vocalist award, she said she was "completely overwhelmed." Then, looking at her husband, who had tears in his eyes, she said, "To my husband, without whom I would be able to do nothing."

Tim lost out for Single of the Year, but he won the award for Top Male Vocalist. When he went to the stage to accept the award, Faith rose to her feet in the audience and applauded. Tim was moved when he spotted Faith standing up for him. "My lovely wife," he said. "I couldn't do anything without you. I love you so much."

When Shania Twain was awarded the top honor of the evening, Entertainer of the Year, Faith was backstage talking to an Associated Press reporter. "I think Tim deserves that award and I am hopeful he will get it sometime," she said. "You can't take anything away from Shania. But it's now time for my husband to win that award!"

If Faith and Tim were not the most in-love couple in show business, they certainly were executing a world-class performance.

Sex sells! *Country Weekly*'s May 30, 2000, edition featured a cover story with a large photo of Faith Hill smiling broadly and glancing over her bare shoulder into the camera lens with a look that seemed to say, *Catch me if you can.* The headline read: "Top Twenty-five Sexiest Stars."

"Country music is baring a lot more than emotions these days," wrote the magazine's editors. "Witness the hunks and hotties who wind your watch, float your boat and start your engines—the ones who push the needle on the ooh-la-la meter into the red. With so many tantalizing faces and bodies to choose from, our list could have gone on forever, so narrowing it to twenty-five was no easy task."

The number one sexiest star in country music—Faith Hill! Coming in second was Shania Twain, with George Strait and Alan Jackson coming in third and fourth respectively (go figure). The Dixie Chicks were not far behind at number seven.

That same month, that bastion of female pulchritude, *Playboy* magazine, declared Faith "Babe of the Month." An accompanying photograph shows Faith squatting in a blue dress, with her skirt pulled aside to show her bare legs. "We're big fans, and we hope we'll have more Faith in the future," wrote the editors.

There is little doubt that Faith Hill is the sexiest woman in country music, but does that mean that she—and the other recording artists branded with that label—are selling sex in lieu of music? To date, neither Faith, Shania, nor the Dixie Chicks have ever appeared nude or even semi-nude in print or video. The hostility the conservative country-music industry has displayed toward Faith has more to do with her assertiveness than any amount of skin she has ever shown in a video or photograph.

If an assertive woman comes onto the country-music scene she is labeled either a slut or a lesbian by the old guard. Regardless of what people say behind her back, Faith has succeeded with the CD-buying public simply by selling herself as she is: a slender woman with a striking face who has a voice to die for. If she is sexy, she believes, it is because God made her that way.

Sex clearly sells in country music, but only when it is perceived to be something other than sex. The millions of female album-buyers who have made superstars out of Faith and Shania are not buying their albums because they are attracted to them sexually, but because they perceive the entertainers' message to be one that applies to them. Faith and Shania are role models for women who want to develop their own sexuality.

The country-music industry is still struggling to cope with this new phenomenon. At its May 2000 gathering, the Country Radio Seminar attempted, without much success, to deal with dueling research reports and male program directors that expressed outright hostility to the "soft" sound promoted by female recording artists.

Traditionally, many radio stations drop country artists from their playlists if their songs cross over to pop radio. They do that to punish the recording artists. One researcher at the conference—which incidentally was attended by Faith Hill—told the executives that they should continue playing songs that cross over because the songs act as commercials for country music in general. Some radio programmers in the audience voiced concern that it would damage the "purity" of the music if they played songs that also were airing on pop stations. Another researcher warned that all the "soft" music being recorded by female artists was alienating male listeners.

While it is true that country radio may be in trouble, the record companies that record the music and sell it are paying closer attention to the bottom line. Early in 2000, SoundScan, a New York–based company that tracks music sales around the country, reported that country-music sales were down nearly 5 percent.

Those lowered sales come at a time when the top-selling country album for both 1998 and 1999 was Shania Twain's *Come On Over*. No one likes lower sales, but data like that only convinces the record companies that they need more, not less music of the type recorded by Faith and Shania.

The changes brought about in the music industry by the music of Faith and Shania were shadowed at the local level in Nashville by a change in ownership of the TNN Music Awards. Founded in 1967 by *Music City News*, a Nashville-based magazine devoted entirely to country music, the TNN awards are similar to those presented by the Academy of Country Music and the Country Music Association. For the first twenty years of its existence, the awards were a low-key imitation of the major awards; then, about ten years ago, the magazine joined forces with The Nashville Network (TNN), a merger which gave the event a higher profile and its name, the TNN Music Awards.

All that changed in the summer of 1999, when TNN declined to renew its contract with *Music City News*. The magazine went out of business and TNN affiliated with a new publication, *Country Weekly*. With that merger, came a new name: *Country Weekly* Presents the TNN Awards.

With a new name and a new format, the awards show was held on June 15, 2000, at Nashville's Gaylord Entertainment Center. Faith and Tim attended the live telecast, both dressed in Johnny Cash black. Faith was nominated for an astonishing eight awards: Entertainer of the Year, Female Artist of the Year, Collaborative Event, Album of the Year, Song of the Year, Single of the Year, Video of the Year, and the "Impact" award, for "presence in film, television, commercials or soundtracks."

Faith beat out Shania Twain, Jo Dee Messina, Martina McBride, and Reba McEntire for the Female Artist award, but she lost the Entertainer of the Year, Album of the Year, Single of the Year, Song of the Year, Collaborative Event of the Year, Video of the Year, and the Impact award to George Strait, who seemed to be the favorite country entertainer of the year among the contest's voters.

Backstage, Messina told *Country Weekly* that she wished all the contest voters could get to know Faith personally. "She's like a walking angel," she said. "She really is one of the greatest creatures God put upon this earth."

⟶ When Tim, Faith, and their two children arrived at Ralph Wilson Stadium in Orchard Park, New York, a suburb of Buffalo, they had no reason to think that it would be anything other than a routine visit. It was June 2000 and Tim and close friend Kenny Chesney were two of the opening acts for the George Strait Country Music Festival. Faith and the children were just along for the ride. Their plan was to hang out at the bus while Tim performed.

The quality that had most attracted Faith to Tim, his gentle manner with children, had been confirmed in her eyes a week earlier, when he was chosen Father of the Year by the National Fatherhood Initiative at a ceremony in Washington, D.C. Created in 1994 by former United States education secretary William Bennett, actor James Earl Jones, and pollster George Gallup, the NFI's mission is to combat the growing problem of fatherlessness by restoring responsible fatherhood as a national priority.

The day that Faith sat in the audience and watched Tim receive his award as Father of the Year was among the proudest in her life. She wept openly as the man she had chosen to father her children was recognized for his understanding and compassion.

Faith understood all too well the emotional toll of growing up fatherless. It is true that she had a loving adoptive father, whom she loved and respected, but that did not entirely negate the hollowness, the guilt, the hurt that comes from not having a relationship with one's natural father. Tim already stood tall in Faith's eyes—the award transformed him into a giant.

When the trouble started at the concert, Faith and the girls were inside the tour bus. Tim and Chesney were outside the arena, in the parking area for the tour buses and equipment trucks. It was blocked off from the public so the equipment would not be vandalized or tampered with.

Security and traffic control for the concert were supplied by deputies from the Erie County Sheriff's Department. By the time Tim and Chesney performed, however, the deputies were on break. The deputies had their routine down pat. They were needed most before and after the concert, when traffic was circulating around the stadium. During the concert, they faded into the background. They had done it hundreds of times before. Although during the summer months the stadium mostly was used for concerts, during the fall and winter it was used by the Buffalo Bills NFL football team for their home games.

The first thing Tim and Chesney saw when they went outside was a couple of horses used by the mounted division of the sheriff's department. The mounted officers worked part-time for the sheriff's department and they owned their own horses. Tim and Chesney approached the horses, which were being held by the thirty-five-year-old daughter of one of the deputies. The officers were all in a nearby building, attending a training session conducted by the sheriff's department.

Chesney is not your typical country-music singer. Born in east Tennessee, he grew up with a rustic, idealized concept of country music—not an uncommon attitude in that part of the state. He decided he wanted to go into country music while attending college, but he didn't do anything rash like dropping out of school. He picked up a degree in marketing before moving to Nashville in 1990 to try his hand as a songwriter.

It took five years of hard work for Chesney to land a record contract with a major label. Now, five years after the release of his first album, he was out on the road with two of his heroes, Tim McGraw and George Strait.

Chesney has several distinctive qualities, but perhaps the most prominent is this Opie Taylor air he has about him. Back in the 1960s, he would have fit in nicely on *The Andy Griffith Show*. By 2000 standards, he was about as far away from the "outlaw" label as a country singer could be. He once confided to this author that his most embarrassing moment occurred in the third grade, when he was kissed by a smitten classmate, an unexpected act of affection that caused him to pee in his pants.

When Chesney saw the horses, he approached them, Opie-like, and asked the woman holding them if he could sit atop one of the horses. She said yes, and that is where the story took an ugly turn, for instead of simply sitting on the horse, Chesney dug his imaginary spurs into the horse's flank and took off down the road.

"It was at that point in time, when the deputies were coming out of the training session, that the deputy who owned the horse saw [what was happening], saying to the other deputies, 'Hey! That's my horse. Stop him!'" said Erie County Sheriff Patrick Gallivan. Two deputies jumped into a car and drove over to where Chesney, by that time, had stopped the horse, according to Gallivan.

While Chesney remained in the saddle the way motorists are advised to stay in the driver's seat when pulled over, the two deputies got out of the patrol car to talk to him. It was at that point, when the second deputy was walking around the car, that Tim McGraw appeared, seemingly from nowhere.

Approaching the deputy from behind, Tim leaped onto the officer's back and put his arm around his neck and head, tightening his grip into what looked like a choke hold. As this was going on, Chesney calmly got down from the horse, offering no resistance to the police. As the second deputy danced around with Tim on his back, other deputies ran to his aid. It was at that point that Tim's road manager, forty-four-year-old Mark Russo, joined in the melee. Within moments the other deputies pulled Tim from the deputy's back. "Once that happened, McGraw squared off with the other deputy in a threatening-type posture, according to one of the deputies, although no additional physical altercation took place," said Gallivan.

Immediately after the altercation, Tim and Chesney retreated to the tour bus (or a nearby trailer) and the deputies reported the incident to department headquarters. "Our supervisors were called in and it took awhile for them to sort things out," said Gallivan. "The deputies did not know that the person on the horse was a performer named Kenny Chesney nor that the guy on the back was another performer. One of our chiefs ended up speaking to one of McGraw's managers. The actual mechanism for McGraw being taken into custody, I don't know exactly how that happened, but he was not yanked away immediately after the shuffle and placed in handcuffs. It was after our person in charge talked with his manager to sort things out."

Tim and Chesney were arrested and taken to a command post at the local fire station, then they were transported in a police van to a judge for arraignment. Tim was charged with second-degree assault (a felony), obstructing governmental administration, and menacing and resisting arrest. Chesney was cited for disorderly conduct. Tim, Chesney, and Russo all pleaded not guilty. The judge set Tim's bond at $2,500 and Chesney's at $100. Both men were released on bail pending further court appearances.

Gallivan said he considers the charges against Tim serious because of what it represents: "The felony charge did not have to do with the seriousness of the injury, but rather the fact that an assault upon a police officer in New York is a felony."

Tim's arrest made headlines nationwide, but nowhere was the news more devastating than in Nashville, where Tim and Faith were accustomed to being treated like music royalty. Tim's arrest sent a shudder along Music Row. It was not the kind of publicity country music needed.

Especially hard-hit was Tim's record label, Curb Records, where the straitlaced Mike Curb encouraged his artists to be good role models. Mike did not issue any personal statement about the arrest, but few observers had any doubts about what the Bush Republican thought about the incident. Here was a man, remember, that dropped recording acts from his record label over the drug-use issue. The only unanswered question was what he planned to do about Tim.

Once the story broke, Chesney was the first to respond. "Unfortunately, what was meant to be a totally innocent and fun gesture was blown way out of proportion," he said in a written statement. On Jay Leno's *Tonight Show* he said the incident was like a scene from the 1970s cop show *Starsky and Hutch*: "The guy in the driver's seat just slid over the hood, and they started pulling me off." Asked why he was riding the horse in the first place, Chesney said he was taking it into the backstage area to show the other performers' children.

The incident put Tim and Faith in turmoil—"Father of the Year Jumps Cop" was not the type of headline that made Faith teary-eyed with admiration. It took almost a week for Tim to issue a statement giving his side of the incident. He said he intervened only because he saw police officers trying to "rip" Chesney from the horse. "At no time did I throw any punches or put anyone in anything remotely resembling a choke hold. One of the officers pulled his nightstick and hit me at least three times on my leg."

Tim said he was motivated to intervene because he thought his friend was in danger, and because his children were playing nearby under Faith's supervision and he feared for their safety. Asked if there was any validity to Tim's claim that he had acted to protect his wife and children, Gallivan said that he was certain no children or bystanders had been in danger at any time. "The police car was not driven recklessly, it was driven only a short distance," he said. "There was no reason for anyone to think that bystanders or children were in jeopardy."

Nashville is a city of deals—record deals, publishing deals, movie deals, television deals . . . deals on cars, homes, and horses . . . deals on guitars, women, and drugs—so Tim's arrest naturally became a big deal. No one stopped to ask, *What was he thinking?* Instead, everyone asked, *What's the deal with this deal?*

Tim's manager, Scott Siman, told *Tennessean* columnist Brad Schmitt that Tim had had a right to intervene. He compared it to intervening in the Rodney King beating. His choicest words were directed toward Sheriff Gallivan, who he said has been "outrageous in the deal. The guy's had more press conferences than Tim has had."

As the summer wore on, Tim's attorneys were successful in getting the felony assault charge reduced to misdemeanor assault. Even so, a conviction could result in considerable jail time for Tim. A trial date was set for December 6, 2000.

Perhaps seeing an opportunity to get a deal out of the deal, Tim's lawyers responded to the arrests with notice of intent to file a lawsuit against the sheriff's department for "false arrest, malicious prosecution, unlawful imprisonment, use of excessive force, assault, negligence, reck-lessness, carelessness, libel, slander and constitutional rights violations."

Sheriff Gallivan has received numerous letters, telephone calls, and e-mails voicing support for the singer, but he says that public support for the deputies has been "overwhelming." Says Gallivan: "The fans say [they] have been fans of Tim McGraw for X number of years and [they] know he would never do anything like that. And these are people . . . who have never met the man. They have no way of knowing what his personality is or what he is capable of or isn't capable of. . . . There are those who think it has been blown out of proportion, but I guess you get that anytime you have a controversial issue, with people on two sides of the issue."

There may have been two sides to the issue, but Faith Hill never wavered from the side she thought was correct: "That story got blown way out of proportion," she said. "Tim was coming to the defense of a friend."

A little over three weeks after the incident in New York, Faith and Tim made a joint concert appearance in Jackson, Mississippi, at—of all places—the Jackson Zoo. The July 1 concert was a benefit performance to raise money for the zoo's education center. Faith's brother Wesley recently had been named director of the center, and she felt obligated to help him out in his efforts to raise money for a new building.

"I'm very proud that my brother is so passionate about this," Faith told Gary Pettus, a staff writer with Jackson's only morning newspaper, the *Clarion Ledger*. "It's coming from his heart. He wants this education center to happen, in a big way. It all starts with someone who has a dream and believes in it. That's why I believe he is so important in making it happen."

The zoo printed up five thousand tickets. They sold out quickly, however, and more had to be printed. By the time Faith took the stage at six o'clock, the temperature was a stifling ninety degrees and a crowd estimated by police to exceed ten thousand was packed onto the zoo grounds. Many people brought lawn chairs and blankets, setting up camp with ice coolers and baskets containing fried chicken, fresh tomatoes, and both banana and chocolate Moon Pies.

Most of the people in the audience were female, but men of all ages were well represented. Among the men present was Vance Dyess, a retired Baptist preacher who had attended the Star Baptist Church when Faith was a member of the congregation. He wore a starched white shirt and dress slacks, looking every bit the retired servant of the Lord. Unfortunately, he had encountered a run of bad luck in recent years, developing multiple sclerosis and even more recently breaking his leg. He sat in a wheelchair, his broken right leg elevated for support.

"Faith is such a precious person," he said. "She has friends by the multitude. What we like about Faith is that she talks about Star, Mississippi. I was her favorite preacher for a while. I was not her pastor, but I was her favorite preacher. She was kind to everyone. Everyone was her friend."

Although uncomfortable and obviously in some pain, Brother Dyess had a blissful look on his face. "Being in a wheelchair and having multiple sclerosis, I never know how it is going to be. This heat is going to make me so weak; I will be weak for a week, but I was determined to see her."

At Brother Dyess's feet was a large sign with handwritten letters that said, FAITH, BROTHER DYESS. He planned to hold the sign up when Faith took the stage. He explained: "I'm hoping she will see it and throw me a kiss!"

Not far away from Brother Dyess was a small group of Faith's friends from McLaurin High School, including Terry Moody and Adrienne Massey Cooley. "I think it is great that she would come here and do this for her brother and for the zoo," said Moody. A round of "amens" went around the group, making it clear that Faith was more than just another classmate to them.

"We knew she could do it," said Cooley, a former McLaurin High homecoming queen who still has the looks to land a title or two. "She has a good head on her shoulders. I appreciate how she and Tim portray such a positive image of a good marriage. I think that is good to let people know you can have a good marriage. It's good to let people see that you can be faithful to each other. That is a radical concept for country music."

The closer it came to concert time, the more restless the overheated crowd became. People started pushing, shoving. Those seated on blankets were soon overwhelmed by the simple weight of the crowd as it pushed closer to the stage. A young girl standing near Brother Dyess fainted and fell to the ground, creating a buzz of hysteria among her friends until paramedics arrived and gave her oxygen.

A rather nasty fight broke out among two warring factions of women, each pushing and elbowing to occupy the same space. "You want a piece of this?" yelled out one woman in her early twenties. She held her fist menacingly in the air, her jaw clenched and her face covered with sweat. "I'll kick your ass!"

"You won't kick nobody's ass," yelled out the woman who was the object of the threat. She stamped her foot, sending a child seated on a blanket nearby into tears. "You want to see some ass-kickin', you just come on ahead!"

Throughout it all, Brother Dyess retreated into the sanctity of his thoughts.

Suddenly, without warning, Tim McGraw took the stage wearing a white, broad-brimmed cowboy hat, a white T-shirt, dark sunglasses, and blue jeans. To the delight of some of the women near the stage, he opened the show, singing several of his hits.

Assaulted by a heat index of one hundred, Tim looked hot and tired, his face clearly showing the tension of the past several weeks. On his trip to the stage, he couldn't help but notice that the concert was patrolled by dozens of mounted officers, all of whom looked sullen and humorless atop their horses.

Tim knew as well as anyone how Mississippians felt about people who jumped on police officers—they were either drug-crazed hippies or white-trash roustabouts. If Tim had heard the concertgoer yell out at one of the mounted officers—"Hey, you better not let Tim get near that horse!"—and if he had seen the grim expression on the police officer's face, he would have been horrified.

Tim was a great opening act, but he was no Faith Hill. When the star of the show finally ran out onto the stage, the crowd of ten thousand roared, sending out a wave of sound that surely must have caught her attention with the sheer force of its impact.

Dressed in a white pullover shirt and red slacks, she wore her hair pulled back away from her face and anchored in place with a blue bandanna. Dark sunglasses protected her eyes from the intense white heat that hit the stage with a fury. Clearly Faith was in no mood for fancy stage outfits or glamour-girl pretense. She was among home folks. She knew they would understand.

From the moment she stepped out in front of the band, one thing was clear: Faith was in control of the stage. Typically female country singers are at the mercy of their male band members while performing onstage; most try to keep up with the band, not the other way around. One of the most surprising things about Faith Hill is the way in which her performance personality runs counter to her soft-focus television and video image. From the first note of her first song—"This Kiss"—she set the pace and the band and her trio of background singers struggled to keep up with her.

Not far into the first song, Brother Dyess held up his sign with one hand and with the other blew kisses to Faith, his arm arching out away from his lips with a grand gesture that wouldn't have been any more impressive had he been trying to get the attention of Jesus Christ himself. Spotting the sign, Faith gave him a thumbs-up and then acknowledged him once she completed the song. She never blew him a kiss, which must have disappointed him, but then, she did not send out kisses to anyone else, either.

After several songs, Faith paused so that a representative from the mayor's office could come onstage and present her brother Wesley with the city's inaugural "Best of the New South" award for his work with the Jackson Zoo. Embarrassed by the attention, Wesley accepted the award—and a hug from his sister—then exited with an awe-shucks mumble to the crowd and big cotton-row strides that got him offstage in seconds flat.

Faith sang several more songs, wrapping the crowd around her finger as she pranced back and forth across the stage, displaying a level of musical energy that must be seen in person to be appreciated. For the encore, Tim joined Faith onstage to sing their number one duet, "It's Your Love."

By the time the concert ended, sunset was approaching. Wild jungle screams and chatters could be heard in the distance from the animals, who were not accustomed to large crowds and high-powered speaker systems. As the crowd of ten thousand filtered out of the zoo, a man carrying a lawn chair put his arm around his female companion. "Those are my kind of people," he said, referring to Faith and Tim.

⌐ Eleven days after the Jackson concert, Faith and Tim kicked off their twenty-three-city "Soul2Soul" tour at the Phillips Arena in Atlanta. The venue was sold out, but so many people showed up at the arena looking for tickets that the promoters opened up the seating behind the stage and packed it with grateful fans.

Faith and Tim had toured together before they married, but this was their first tour as husband and wife. With Gracie and Maggie traveling in the bus with them, it truly was a family affair. Almost from day one in the marriage, Faith had imposed a rule that both of them vowed never to break: Under no circumstances would they ever allow themselves to spend more than three days at a time apart.

Accompanying Faith on the tour was the fifth member of the family— her makeup kit. This was no tote-and-run plastic case filled with lipstick and blush-on. It was a huge, three-hundred-pound case on seven wheels that was designed specifically for her. It contains sixteen-inch drawers, several mirrors, padded shelves, and a light with a timer that shuts off the lights in case Faith leaves in a hurry. Reportedly, it cost over $4,000 to construct. That sounds like a lot of money, but it is only chump change if you believe reports that she pays hair and makeup pros $5,000 per show to help her look her best.

The Soul2Soul tour did so well on its first leg that it was extended until mid-December. According to Pollstar, a firm that tracks concert revenues, it was the largest-grossing country tour of the summer, taking in more than $18 million on its first leg. By the time the second and third legs were added to the tour, they had grossed over $45 million in sixty-four cities, playing to an estimated one million fans—not bad for a couple of starry-eyed kids from the Deep South.

In September, Faith took a short break from the tour to record her first holiday song, titled "Where Are You Christmas?" Penned by James Horner, Will Jennings, and Mariah Carey, it is featured in the Jim Carrey movie *Dr. Seuss' How the Grinch Stole Christmas*. A few weeks later, she shot a video for the song.

In October, a little over two months before the Soul2Soul tour ended, Faith and Tim pulled the buses and big rigs off the road long enough to attend the 2000 Country Music Association Awards in Nashville. It had been seven years since the release of her first album, so the question on everyone's mind was whether she would once again be shut out for an award. The three CMAs she *had* won hardly counted—Vocal Event of the Year, Song of the

Year, Video of the Year—since the first was really an award for Tim and the other two were awards to her songwriter and her video director.

In 2000, Faith was nominated for five awards: Entertainer of the Year, Female Vocalist of the Year, Vocal Event of the Year (for her duet with Tim, "Let's Make Love"), Single of the Year, Album of the Year, and Video of the Year. Practically shadowing his wife, Tim was nominated for three awards: Entertainer of the Year, Male Vocalist of the Year, and Vocal Event of the Year.

Faith opened the show with a high-energy performance of "There Will Come a Day." With her onstage were nearly two dozen African-Americans in black choir robes, singing, clapping, and dancing about the stage with Faith. With its nod to gospel, rhythm and blues, and African-American inspiration, the performance was anathema to everything the "old" country music stood for.

When the camera panned the audience it showed Tim on his feet, proudly applauding. Sadly, he was practically the only person in the audience giving her a standing ovation. The next morning, the Nashville *Tennessean* sniffed that the performance was "more about selling the smoke-swathed dance number than the personal, emotional stories traditionally associated with country music."

Surprisingly, master of ceremonies Vince Gill, a longtime friend of Faith Hill and one of the genuine good guys of country music, took the stage immediately after her performance and commented, "Man . . . pretty tough to look at." It was a backhanded compliment and the normally good-hearted Vince knew it, for he quickly added: "It's been an incredible year for Faith Hill. Let's give her another round of applause. I think she's nominated for everything, and deservedly so."

Later in the show, Tim performed a song that he felt strongly about, "Things Change." It is a song about how country music has to change in order to grow. It was a ringing endorsement of Faith's efforts to carry country music to the next level. Whatever Tim's shortcomings, it could never be said he did not stand tall for his wife.

"Good job, Timmy," Vince said after the performance. "I forgot to mention one thing about Tim—he'll be starring in an episode of *COPS* with Kenny 'Puffy' Chesney." It was said in good jest, and although the camera did not pick up Tim's reaction, he was probably smiling.

As the various awards were presented, it looked as if Faith would once again be ignored by the CMA. The Dixie Chicks won in the album category; Lee Ann Womack got Single of the Year; George Strait and Alan Jackson took home the award for Vocal Event. Faith was quickly running out of possibilities. There were only three categories left: Female Vocalist, Male Vocalist, and Entertainer of the Year.

When the winner for Male Vocalist was announced, not many people in the audience were surprised that the award went to Tim. Over the past two years he had developed into a real powerhouse, outshining such veterans as George Strait and Clint Black.

Before going to the stage, Tim kissed Faith. "First off, I want to say hi to Gracie and Maggie," he said, cradling the award. "I know you guys are getting tired of hearing this, but—To my soul mate and my wife, who is my inspiration I couldn't do anything without, I love you."

Nominated along with Faith for Female Vocalist were Tim's protégée Jo Dee Messina, Martina McBride, Lee Ann Womack, and Trisha Yearwood. When the winner was announced, Faith looked totally shocked to hear her name called out. After seven years, it was the first CMA award she had ever received for her efforts as a singer.

"Wow! I did not expect to get this award, I tell you," she told the audience. "I feel so alone. My husband's not out here. Can I hug somebody?"

With that, the camera located Tim backstage. Looking like a lovesick schoolboy, he wrapped his arms around himself, hugging his wife in absentia.

"I must say this," Faith continued, her voice more serious now. "Everyone has questioned where I'm at, what I'm doing. And I'll tell you something. I love this industry and I love the people in this business and my heart is here and I work hard. . . . This means a lot to me, but my family means everything to me."

The irony of the tension between the CMA and Faith is only compounded by the success that she and Tim had throughout the year. Add their joint album sales with revenues from their tour and you get a $100 million year, giving them the largest household income in country music.

The only real downside had been Tim's arrest in New York. The effects of that incident on his marriage and career cannot be overemphasized. Tim had blanketed his wife with public adoration from the CMA stage, but once her turn came, Faith was more interested in making a statement to the CMA than to her husband. She didn't seem the same with Tim that evening. There was a remoteness in her eyes that made her seem distant.

Following the arrest, Tim began having problems with his record label. Was the superconservative Mike Curb going to punish Tim for embarrassing the label? Publicly Curb stood behind Tim, but what was happening behind the scenes signaled a different message. "Things Change," the new single Tim debuted at the CMA awards, had not been released yet, nor would it be that year.

Inexplicably, Curb decided to put a hold on Tim's new album, the one containing the single "Things Change." Instead Curb decided to release a greatest-hits album. That decision made Tim furious and he was not shy about telling reporters that he felt mistreated by Curb.

In the days following the CMA telecast, copies of "Things Change" began popping up at radio stations around the country. Within days the song was on the national charts. Tim denied he had anything to do with the song's release. In a statement issued by his publicist, he surmised that "unknown fans" had taped the song from the telecast and then posted it on Napster, the Internet company that allows visitors to its site to post recordings that can be downloaded by anyone who wants a copy.

That explanation sounded plausible, but when taped copies of the song started appearing at radio stations in Nashville, the trail led to Tim or Curb, the most likely sources for the mystery tapes. Both Curb and Tim's manager, Scott Siman, denied they were the source of the tapes. "We're pretty proud of ourselves, but I'm not that clever," Siman told country.com writer Edward Morris.

Curb Records told reporters that "Things Change" might not even be on Tim's next album. Was this a not-so-subtle message to Tim that he should cool it if he wanted the song on the album? The public argument with Tim over his next album was embarrassing, but it was the least of the record label's worries. Its top female star, LeAnn Rimes, had filed a federal lawsuit in Dallas against Curb Records, seeking to negate the contract her parents had signed with the company when she was twelve. Her attorney said his client was not suggesting that the record company had taken advantage of her, merely that Rimes thought she could do better at another company.

Rimes had already sued her father, charging that he had mismanaged her career. At about the time that LeAnn sued Curb Records, she was countersued by her father, who depicted his daughter as out of control. He alleged that his daughter, when she was fifteen, had been in "constant companionship" with a forty-year-old man. He called her "a spoiled brat."

Mike Curb disappeared from public view—and who could blame him? His top male star was in trouble with the police and his top female star was suing to get out of her contract with him and, even worse, carrying on a public feud with her father that was beginning to look more salacious than anything ever dreamed up on daytime television. These were not the types of things a Bush Republican wanted on his résumé.

Faith managed to stay out of Tim's spat with his record label, but she did not manage to stay out of trouble. She injured her foot playing softball at her husband's annual Swampstock event in Louisiana. The injury occurred while she was going after a line drive. The ball hit her on the ankle, necessitating a trip to the hospital. Luckily, no bones were broken, but the injury meant that she would end October on crutches.

Faith's injury was the first medical emergency of the year, but it was not the last. Soon Tim would have a medical emergency of his own.

Even as the Soul2Soul tour continued, new opportunities were coming Faith's way. CBS Television, responding to a pitch by Faith's manager Gary Borman, asked the singer to host her own Thanksgiving-evening television special. Since there was no time to put together a show from scratch in a studio, the one-hour special was built around Faith's two-night concert booking at the Palace of Auburn Hills in Auburn Hills, Michigan, just outside Detroit.

Despite a hectic concert schedule, Faith made time to go to New York to promote the television special, appearing on the *Today* show, *Live with Regis*, and *Late Night with David Letterman*. Her New York week began with an early-morning performance on a stage located outside the *Today* show's Studio A in Rockefeller Center.

It was a chilly thirty-eight degrees and Faith had wrapped herself from head to toe in a black knit cap, gloves, black turtleneck sweater, and an ankle-length coat. An adoring audience, largely female, held up large photos of Faith to the cameras and gave her a very warm reception.

After performing two songs—"Breathe" and "The Way You Love Me"—Faith went inside the television studio, where her appearance on the *Today* show took on the character of a family reunion. Six years earlier, her first national television interview had taken place on the *Today* show with then substitute host Matt Lauer. Now he was a full-time co-host and she was a major star.

"Let's go back six years," Lauer said. "You're on this show. I remember vividly because I was nervous. I was filling in for Bryant [Gumbel]. Do you remember that time as being a particularly exciting and nerve-wracking time in your career?"

"It's more exciting now," she said, pausing in a typical Faith moment. *Had she offended him?* "It was exciting talking to you," she continued, laughing. "But my career was so young, so much to do, and you don't know where you fit into all that stuff. I'm much more comfortable in my skin now than I was then."

The next evening she appeared on *Late Night with David Letterman*, following lead-off guest MS-NBC anchor Brian Williams. If she was uneasy being in the hot seat next to Letterman, who has a reputation for giving beautiful women a tough time, she did not show it. Poised and relaxed, she wore a T-shirt that had the word *David* emblazoned across her chest in rhinestones and punctuated with small hearts.

Faith jokingly told the audience that she had found the shirt in Letterman's dressing room. Letterman laughed and asked her if he could have the shirt when she was "finished with it."

The most comical—and the most revealing—part of the interview came when Letterman asked Faith about her children. "Tim and I were talking today and decided that we are not going to educate our children—we don't want them to leave," she said, laughing. "We want to keep them right there so they will never marry, they won't know anything about the world. They won't be able to do anything without us."

Letterman told her that was "backward" thinking, then added that he had been home-schooled.

"That explains a lot," said Faith.

The Thanksgiving special was pretty much as advertised. Sixty minutes of Faith Hill—minus commercials (and there were plenty, including a Cover Girl spot that featured Niki Taylor, not Faith)—in concert, with occasional backstage banter between songs. There were no guest stars, with the exception of Tim, who came onstage to sing their duet "Let's Make Love."

Faith was radiant throughout the concert, displaying a level of self-confidence that was amazing to those who had known her at the start of her career. She sang her major hits, including "This Kiss" and "Breathe," but the song she seemed to put the most emotional involvement into was "What's In It for Me?"

The lead-in to the song was a long monologue during which Faith, working the audience like a tent-show evangelist, talked about male-female relationships. "Everybody's got one," she said. "Whether it be whatever, you got one, right?"

She talked about a woman who awoke one morning to discover that she no longer wanted to put up with the emotional baggage that accompanied her relationship. The result was that she went to her man and said, "I love you so much, but I'm tired. . . . What's in it for me? That's what I want to know."

In the weeks following her Thanksgiving special, Faith racked up even more awards. At the *Billboard* awards she won the "Hot 100 Single of the Year" (for "Breathe"), and at the inaugural *My VH1 Music Awards* she was chosen Woman of the Year, and was given an award in the Sexiest Video category for "Breathe" and an award for her Pepsi advertisements.

When she won the video award, she was shown by remote camera from a concert venue in New Jersey, where she was performing that night. Faith seemed somewhat rattled by the Sexiest Video award and, for a moment, she was almost speechless. Why shouldn't she be? Whoever heard of a country artist winning an award for the "Sexiest" anything, over the likes of competitors Jennifer Lopez, Enrique Iglesias, Sisqó, and D'Angelo? "I don't know what to say, but thanks," she told the audience.

Tim was with Faith at the *Billboard* awards, but only because the Erie County prosecutor had agreed to postpone his December 6 court date so that Tim could be at Faith's side at the Las Vegas awards show.

He had never *not* been with her at such a crucial time. Somehow Tim had been able to convince the prosecutor of the importance of that appearance to his marriage. Two months earlier, when Faith had accepted an award at the Country Music Association telecast, she had looked around the audience and—not seeing Tim—had asked who she could hug. At the time, her comment had seemed nonsensical. In view of Tim's December 6 court date, it now made complete sense. She was well aware of the date for the *Billboard* awards and her comment was a clear message to Tim: Be there, or be in trouble. Luckily for Tim, the prosecutor showed compassion for his plight.

Earlier in the year, long before the incident in New York, rumors had circulated that Tim and Faith's marriage was in trouble. There were also vicious rumors that Maggie was not Tim's child, that Faith was having an affair with her hairdresser, that she was having an affair with her *female* makeup artist!

In an interview with *People* magazine, Faith herself brought up those rumors and, while denying there was any truth to any of them, said: "The naysayers. I don't need their approval. I have too much going on. If that's their entertainment, fine."

Not buying in to the rumors are Faith's many fans. For Diana LeBlanc of New Brunswick, Canada, Faith speaks for the woman "whose heart has been filled with love or squeezed empty by regret."

"To me, she inspires faith in family values," said Steven Foster, a twenty-seven-year-old fan in Northern Ireland. "Which is why so many families come to see her shows. Moreover, her and Tim's image works very well together. Extremely sexy, sensual, and fun. It displays to consumers everywhere the ideal of a wholesome family, and a couple who are atypically the American Dream in every sense of the word—two kids, happy in love, and successful in career."

Faith buys in to that herself, which may be why she is so convincing as an artist. "Without question, my family comes before anything that my career offers," she told *McCall's* magazine. "I know that for me, having both is doable—it just takes knowing how to organize and plan."

During her Thanksgiving special, Faith told the audience that 2000 had been the "most unforgettable" year in her life—and it would be hard to argue with that. At thirty-three, Faith was better than she ever had been before. Her music was soaring, her growth as a woman was inspiring, her communicative skills were expanding, and, even physically, she seemed to grow more beautiful with each passing month, giving credence to the view that self-confidence is an integral ingredient in physical beauty.

The only downside to the year came in mid-December, when Faith and Tim returned to Nashville after wrapping up their Soul2Soul tour in Orlando, Florida. Within days of settling back into the comfortable routine of their family life, Tim complained of stomach pains. Faith rushed him to the Baptist Hospital, where Tim underwent an emergency appendectomy. The surgery went well and the following day he left the hospital to recover at home.

But as fabulous as 2000 was for Faith, the new year promised to be even better, with a new album in the works, a Christmas album, a children's book, and her first flirtation with the motion-picture industry (yes, Faith not only looks like a movie star, she is destined to become one). She began the new year reading movie scripts, making peach cobbler for her daughters (and tomato sandwiches for herself), nursing Tim back to health, and, whenever possible, wearing his favorite outfit of hers—"nothing at all."

If Faith thought she was going to get much of a break in 2001, she was mistaken. On January 7, Faith and Tim attended the People's Choice Awards, where she was awarded the trophy for Favorite Female Musical Performer, beating out country rival Shania Twain and pop rival Britney Spears. The ceremony afforded Faith her first opportunity to show off her new razor cut hairdo. It was shorter and blonder than she had ever worn it before—and public reaction to it was not favorable (a poll conducted by *Access Hollywood* disclosed that eighty-nine percent of those who responded disliked the new look).

The following night Faith and Tim attended the American Music Awards, televised live from the Shrine Auditorium in Los Angeles. Nominated in four categories, Faith delighted the audience and home viewers by winning three awards—Favorite Country Album, Favorite Country Female Artist, and Favorite Female Pop/Rock Artist. To win the latter, she topped Christina Aguilera, Celine Dion, and Britney Spears, a co-host of the show. Not since 1988 had a country artist so dominated the awards show.

Faith seemed genuinely surprised to win the pop/rock award. "Okay, what is going on?" she said. "I feel like kinda' stingy all of a sudden . . . let's go par-dee!"

Earlier, while accepting the award for Favorite Country Female Artist, she made a very Faithesque remark about a previous performance in which the dancers all wore men's underwear. "I was going to wear my husband's underwear," she joked, "but it had a hole in it!" After the show, she tried to explain the underwear remark by saying that all the pairs of men's underwear that she had ever seen had had holes in it. She said she was just trying to be funny. Overhearing her explanation, Tim good-naturedly asked her exactly how many men's underwear she had seen. Faith stammered an explanation or two, stumbling badly until she found a proper save with, "well, I have two brothers."

Tim was in a good mood because he had learned that his new album, *Set This Circus Down*, would be released in April and would include the single, "Things Change," which had been the object of so much contention between him and his record label. Mike Curb may have been unhappy with Tim's arrest in New York, but, to his credit, he did not allow it to affect his professional relationship with Tim.

However, by February 21, 2001, the arrest did threaten to tarnish Faith's attendance at the 43rd Annual Grammy Awards at the Staples Center in Los Angeles. On the very day of the ceremony, while Faith was in rehearsals, Tim's lawyers were in court in New York presenting a motion for dismissal of the charges against him.

Faith may have been thinking about Tim's legal problems when she showed up for rehearsal; the first thing she requested was a Tylenol tablet for a headache. Wearing jeans and a black knit shirt, she had her hair pulled back into a miniature ponytail; but her casual appearance did not lessen reaction from backstage personnel, for when she appeared on stage she was greeted by a collective sigh and, later, applause.

With her stunning good looks and glamorous sense of style, Faith had become the people's favorite. Some media critics had proclaimed her too pop to be country—a day or so before she left for the Grammys, a Nashville newspaper asked, "Is Faith really country?"—but to her fans, country was what *they* said was country. And they are correct, of course: Country music ultimately is defined in the global marketplace.

Later that night, before going onstage to sing her hit "Breathe," Faith learned she had won the first Grammys of her career—one for "Best Country Collaboration with Vocals," for her duet with Tim on "Let's Make Love," and the second for "Best Female Country Vocal." From that point on, the evening only got better for Faith.

The major country award of the evening was for "Best Country Album," for which Faith's *Breathe* was nominated, along with albums by Vince Gill, Alan Jackson, Lee Ann Womack, and Trisha Yearwood. When presenter Dolly Parton announced that Faith had won the award, her third Grammy of the evening, no one seemed more surprised than Faith and Tim, who were seated in the front row of the audience.

Wearing a daring, low-cut, see-through black shirt and black bra, Faith accepted the award by first thanking Parton for being the person to present it to her. "Wow!" Faith said, looking at Parton, " . . . and coming from you! I just admire you so much!"

Faith went on to thank her mother and father for allowing her to attend an Elvis Presley concert at the age of eight. She was in the process of thanking others, when she received a hurry-up signal from producers.

"They're saying please wrap up, but this is my . . . " she sputtered with exasperation. Suddenly looking like the fearless girl of her youth who had tempted the racing locomotives, she stamped her foot in defiance and continued. "I've waited a long time for this award," she explained before finishing her thank-yous, finally ending with, " . . . I love *everybody!*"

Faith dreamed of becoming a star almost from the time she could talk, but when stardom came, it arrived in bits and pieces over a ten-year period that tested her in every way imaginable. It is how she handles that stardom in the years ahead that will determine whether she is able to hold on to the dream. Certainly she has the potential to become a true American icon along the lines of Marilyn Monroe or Barbra Streisand— or even her idol, Elvis Presley. All she has to do is stay true to herself. Of course, that may be the hardest part of all.

Discography

"It Matters to Me"
"Bed of Roses"
"A Man's Home Is His Castle"
"You Can't Lose Me"
"I Can't Do That Anymore"
"A Room in My Heart"
"You Will Be Mine"
"Keep Walkin' On"

1 9 9 8

Faith

Warner Bros. Records

Producers: Faith Hill, Byron Gallimore, Dann Huff

Songs:

"This Kiss"
"You Give Me Love"
"Let Me Let Go"
"Love Ain't Like That"
"Better Days"
"My Wild Frontier"
"The Secret of Life"
"Just to Hear You Say that You Love Me" (with Tim McGraw)
"Me"
"I Love You"
"The Hard Way"
"Somebody Stand by Me"

1 9 9 9

Breathe

Warner Bros. Records

Producers: Faith Hill, Dann Huff, Byron Gallimore

Songs:

"What's in It for Me"
"I Got My Baby"
"Love Is a Sweet Thing"

"Breathe"
"Let's Make Love" (with Tim McGraw)
"It Will Be Me"
"The Way You Love Me"
"If I'm Not in Love"
"Bringing Out the Elvis"
"If My Heart Had Wings"
"If I Should Fall Behind"
"That's How Love Moves"
"There Will Come a Day"

2 0 0 0

Dr. Seuss' How the Grinch Stole Christmas (original motion-picture soundtrack)
Interscope/Warner Bros. Records
Producers: Faith Hill, Byron Gallimore
Song:
   "Where Are You Christmas?"—Faith Hill

Recommended Videos

2 0 0 0

"Let's Make Love"
CD: *Breathe*, Faith Hill with Tim McGraw
Warner Bros. Records
Director: Lili Fini Zanuck
Producer: Lynn Zekanis

"Where Are You Christmas?"—Faith Hill
CD: *Dr. Seuss' How the Grinch Stole Christmas*
   (original motion-picture soundtrack)
Warner Bros. Records
CD: Interscope/Warner Bros. Records
Director: Paul Hunter
Producer: Skot Bradford

1 9 9 9

"The Way You Love Me"
CD: *Breathe*, Faith Hill
Warner Bros. Records
Producer: Mary Ann Tanedo

1 9 9 8

"This Kiss"
CD: *Faith*, Faith Hill
Warner Bros. Records
Director: Steve Goldman
Producer: Susan Bowman

"Let Me Let Go"
CD: *Faith*, Faith Hill
Warner Bros. Records
Director: Peter Nyrdle
Producer: Laura Brown

"The Secret of Life"
CD: *Faith*, Faith Hill
Warner Bros. Records
Director: Steven Goldman
Producer: Tamera Brooks

1 9 9 3

"But I Will"
CD: *Take Me As I Am*, Faith Hill
Warner Bros. Records
Director: Leta Warner
Producer: John Duffin

Awards

2 0 0 1

American Music Awards
Female Country Artist
Country Album
Pop/Rock Female Artist

People's Choice Awards
Favorite Female Musical Performer

2 0 0 0

My VH1 Music Awards
Sexiest Video (for "Breathe")
Woman of the Year
"You Want Fries With that Album," for her Pepsi commercials

Billboard *Awards*
Hot 100 Single of the Year

Academy of Country Music
Music Video of the Year
Top Female Vocalist

Country Music Association
　　Female Vocalist of the Year

Country Weekly *Presents The TNN Music Awards*
　　Female Artist of the Year

1 9 9 9

Academy of Country Music
　　Top Female Vocalist
　　Music Video of the Year

Country Music Association
　　Song of the Year

TNN/Music City News
　　Female Artist of the Year
　　Single of the Year
　　Video of the Year
　　Vocal Collaboration of the Year

1 9 9 8

Academy of Country Music
　　Single of the Year
　　Video of the Year
　　Top Female Vocalist
　　Vocal Event of the Year

Country Music Association
　　Video of the Year

1 9 9 7

Academy of Country Music
　　Single of the Year
　　Song of the Year

Video of the Year
Vocal Event of the Year

Country Music Association
Vocal Event of the Year

1 9 9 5

TNN/Music City News
Star of Tomorrow

1 9 9 3

Academy of Country Music
Top New Female Vocalist

Bibliography

Author Interviews

Mary Bailey (1998)
Renee Bell (1997)
Rick Blackburn (1987)
Bill Buckner (2000)
Charlie Butts (2000)
Robin Byrd (2000)
Deana Carter (1997)
Terri Clark (1997)
Adrienne Massey Cooley (2000)
Vance Dyess (2000)

Steven Foster (2000)
Joe Galante (1988)
Sheriff Patrick Gallivan (2000)
Jackie Granberry (2000)
Terry Moody (2000)
Gary Morris (1989) (This interview donated to the Country Music Hall of Fame.)
Shania Twain (1993 and 1995)
Sidney Wheatley (2000)

Books

Dickerson, James. *Women on Top: The Quiet Revolution That's Rocking the American Music Industry*. New York: Billboard Books, 1998.

Editors of *Sports Illustrated*. *Sports Illustrated 1998 Sports Almanac*. New York: Little, Brown and Co., 1997.

Gubernick, Lisa Rebecca. *Get Hot or Go Home*. New York: St. Martin's Paperbacks, 1993.

Leamer, Laurence. *Three Chords and the Truth*. New York: HarperCollins, 1997.

Mansfield, Brian, and Gary Graff, editors. *MusicHound Country: The Essential Album Guide*. Detroit, Michigan: Visible Ink Press, 1997.

Moses, Robert, Alicia Potter, and Beth Rowen, editors. *A&E Entertainment Almanac*. Boston and New York: Houghton Mifflin Company, 1996.

Stambler, Irwin, and Grelun Landon. *The Encyclopedia of Folk, Country and Western Music*. New York: St. Martin's Press, 1984.

Trimble, Betty. *Tim McGraw: A Mother's Story*. Eggman Publishing, 1996.

Magazine and Newspaper Articles

Ansariyah-Grace, Tasneem. "Anthem singer Hill keeping the faith." Nashville *Tennessean*, January 30, 2000.

Bandy, Julie G. "Ladies lead the way as sales soar." *Country Weekly*, March 2, 1999.

Bane, Michael. "Faith Hill." *Country Music*, March/April 1998.

Brown, Jessica. "A real commercial success." *New York Times* News Service, September 2, 2000.

Burrows, Jane. "History of the spit." *Smith County Reformer*, June 23, 1982.

Cooper, Peter. "Hot licks in the country." Nashville *Tennessean*, October 5, 2000.

———. "McGraw may face prison in assault case." Nashville *Tennessean*, June 6, 2000.

———. "McGraw's spokesmen give his side of arrest." Nashville *Tennessean*, June 16, 2000.

Cruz, Clarissa, and Will Lee. "Diva-ster." *Entertainment Weekly*, Summer Movie Double 2000.

Frey, Jennifer. "A Curtain Call in Atlanta." *Washington Post*, August 5, 1996.

Froelich, Paula. *New York Post*, March 28, 2000.

Griffiths, John. " 'I know how lucky I am.' " *McCall's*, November 2000.

Hatt, Holley. "Hill wows fans." *Hastings Tribune*, July 23, 1998.

Havighurst, Craig. "Country puts its pop face forward." Nashville *Tennessean*, October 5, 2000.

———. "Dixie Chicks grab CMA's top honors." Nashville *Tennessean*, October 5, 2000.

Helligar, Jeremy, and Lorna Grisby. "Tim McGraw Biography." *People Profiles*, People.com, October 28, 2000.

Hochman, Steve. "Country hit 'Indian Outlaw' hits a nerve." *Los Angeles Times*, March 24, 1994.

Hitts, Robert. "I made you a star . . ." *Star*, October 17, 1995.

Holden, Larry. "Loving somebody." *Country Weekly*, November 28, 2000.

Huhn, Mary. "Diana Ross: The definition of a diva." *New York Post*, April 4, 2000.

Jerome, Jill. "Road thrill." *People*, August 21, 2000.

Keel, Beverly. "The man nobody knows." *Nashville Scene*, October 2, 1997.

Lasswell, Mark. "Country's better half." *TV Guide*, September 19–25, 1997.

Lawson, Richard. "Bluebird spreads wings." Nashville *Tennessean*, June 6, 2000.

———. "Crossover country songs vital, research suggest." Nashville *Tennessean*, March 3, 2000.

———. "Country's soft side alienates men, study says." Nashville *Tennessean*, March 4, 2000.

McCall, Michael. "Alan Jackson." *Pulse*, November 1996.

———. "Letter from Nashville." *Los Angeles Times*, January 14, 1996.

Morden, Darryl. "Women rule." *Hollywood Reporter*, September 19, 1997.

———. "Crossing over." *Hollywood Reporter*, April 21, 1998.

Morris, Edward. "Pat Quigley leaves Capitol Nashville . . ." country.com, July 17, 2000.

———. "LeAnn Rimes' father hits back at her suit against him."

———. " 'Things Change'—but the questions keep coming." Country.com, November 17, 2000.

Nash, Alanna. "Best of 2000: Faith Hill." *Entertainment Weekly*, December 22–29, 2000.

Newcomer, Wendy. "Women taking country by storm." *Country Weekly*, April 6, 1999.

———. "Tim McGraw on track for his 'place in the sun.' " *Country Weekly*, May 1, 1999.

———. "Setting the record straight." *Country Weekly*, September 19, 2000.

———. "Baring souls." *Country Weekly*, July 11, 2000.

Orr, Jay. "McGraw, Hill kiss in new year." Nashville *Tennessean*, January 1, 2000.

———. "Faith prevails." Country.com, November 22, 2000.

Overstreet, Dianne. "Truly Raleigh's finest." *Smith County Reformer*, June 29, 1983.

Pettus, Gary. "Bring the Faith home, brother." Jackson *Clarion Ledger*, June 1, 2000.

Peyser, Marc. "Beyond cute." *Newsweek*, November 13, 2000.

Pond, Neil. "Most likely to succeed." *Country America*, March 1993.

Roland, Tom. "Hill wins dispute with CMA." Nashville *Tennessean*, September 22, 1999.

———. "CMA awards show rift opens." Nashville *Tennessean*, September 14, 1999.

———. "A new spin at CMA awards." Nashville *Tennessean*, September 25, 1997.

———. "And the makeover awards goes to . . ." Nashville *Tennessean*, June 15, 2000.

———. "Repeat winners top ACMs." Nashville *Tennessean*, May 4, 2000.

Roos, John. *Los Angeles Times* (undated).

Rottenberg, Josh. "Leap of Faith." *US Weekly*, May 15, 2000.

Samuels, Allison. "Worrying about Whitney." *Newsweek*, April 10, 2000.

Schilling, Mary Kaye. "Next big country diva: Faith Hill." *Entertainment Weekly*, February 18, 1994.

Schmitt, Brad. "Brad about you." Nashville *Tennessean*, May 1, 1999.

Schoemer, Karen. "The malling of Shania." *Newsweek*, February 26, 1996.

Schoenfein, Liza. "Runaway Twain." *Entertainment Weekly*, August 11, 1995.

Snow, Donnie. "Faithful sweat it out for stars Hill, Tim McGraw." Jackson *Clarion Ledger*, July 2, 2000.

Tank, Ron. "Hill climbs charts once again." CNN, May 11, 1998.

Tucker, Ken. "Babe in Opryland." *Entertainment Weekly*, August 11, 1995.

Waldman, Alan. "Something old, something new." *Hollywood Reporter*, September 19, 1997.

Willman, Chris. "About Faith." *Entertainment Weekly*, December 10, 1999.

Wix, Kimmy. "Thirty-first Annual CMA Awards Show." Country.com, September 24, 1997.

Wolf, Jeanne. "Keeping the Faith." *Redbook*, June 2000.

(unsigned). "It's still the 'highlight' . . ." *Smith County Reformer*, June 23, 1982.

(unsigned). "No dampened spirits at this year's spit." *Smith County Reformer*, June 30, 1982.

(unsigned). "Spotlight: Faith Hill." Nashville *Tennessean*, October 2, 1994.

(unsigned). "Faith's new hills." *Globe*, October 31, 1995.

(unsigned). "Country's 25 sexiest stars." *Country Weekly*, May 30, 2000.

(unsigned). "Babe of the Month." *Playboy*, May 2000.

(unsigned). "Singers McGraw and Chesney arrested in horse-swiping tiff." *Associated Press*, June 5, 2000.

(unsigned). "Country star McGraw in assault rap." *Associated Press*, June 16, 2000.

(unsigned). "Singer Chesney recalls horse ride." *Associated Press*, June 13, 2000.
(unsigned). "The 50 Most Beautiful People in the World." *People*, April 28, 2000.

Television

VH1 biography: *Behind the Music (Faith Hill)*
Faith Hill CBS Thanksgiving Special (November 23, 2000)
Late Show with David Letterman (November 2000)
The Rosie O'Donnell Show (December 1998)

Court Documents

Audrey Faith Perry Hill v. Daniel Sawyer Hill, no. 93D-2770, Fourth Circuit Court
   for Davidson County, Nashville, Tennessee.